# Don't Trip Over the
# Pebbles in Your Path

*Helen Patrina Stepper*

Veroníka Press
PO Box 1059, Ocean Shores, WA 98569

ISBN (paperback): 0-9661622-0-X

Editorial and design assistance provided by Griffith Publishing, Caldwell, Idaho

DON'T TRIP OVER THE

# PEBBLES IN
# YOUR PATH

### by Roni Bissett
### illustrated by Penny Hale

Published by Veroníka Press

This book belongs to_____

## Dedication

To my children, for their love, encouragement
and support, throughout the process of getting
this book into print—
Gilbert, Leonard, Linda,
Gary, Barbara and Steven.

# Table of Contents

*Dennis G. Smith, Ph.D., Seattle, is the Sno-
homish County Coordinator for Lutheran
Social Services of Washington, Idaho; the
Northwest Regional President for the American Association of Pastoral Counselors,
and is an active pastoral counselor providing individual, marriage and family counseling in the Seattle area since 1984. Dr.
Smith and Roni Bissett worked on the same
counseling staff in Seattle (Puget Counseling Center) from 1984 to 1991. If you need
to contact Dr. Smith, you can reach him at
Lutheran Social Services (425) 672-6009
ext. 350*

# Foreword

Facing a life transitional moment in her mid-forties, Roni Bissett could have played it safe. She had her home in Seattle, her six children were grown, and she held a secure, responsible position at a local hospital. Instead she embarked on a whole new adventure, one which saw her enter and complete college, earn a Master's Degree in Psychology and have a very successful counseling practice.

She became a newspaper advice-columnist, designed and built a retreat center in Ocean Shores, WA. to which people from all over the Pacific Northwest travel in order to participate in her various workshops and retreats.

How did she do it? She did it with wisdom, courage, a firm belief in the goodness and potential of life and the willingness to take charge of her own life-adventure. Through her study, her thousands of hours of direct counseling experience, and her own innate inner wisdom, Roni has learned much about the meaning and purpose of life and how to bring a sense of richness and fullness to the living out of one's life. Her wisdom is grounded in deep common sense, an appreciation of all people and a total belief in the ultimate goodness and potential of the life journey.

This book overflows with her insights and advice for daily living. It covers a variety of subjects from increasing one's self esteem, raising healthy, happy children to enjoying one's senior years with energy and continued growth. It is not advice from an ivory tower but is extremely helpful insights taken from a life well-lived and from the depths of the therapeutic process. Roni knows that the advice and suggestions in this book work, for she has successfully lived each page of this book herself.

—Dennis G. Smith, Ph.D.

# Acknowledgments

I wish to thank all the members of my family, my friends, colleagues, clients and students for their continued love and support, and for their sense of excitement about seeing this book in print—especially my sister, Alice Wegner, for brainstorming with me to come up with a title, and my daughter Barbara for managing the marketing end of this endeavor.

Also I wish to thank Penny Hale for her beautiful illustrations and editing of the original manuscript and Joyce Griffith of Griffith Publishing for her wonderful, insightful assistance in the final editing and formatting of both the book and to Miriam Griffith for her artistic touch with the cover design. A profound thank you to the late Betty Schmitt for her friendship, encouragement and for her reading and comments on my draft manuscript.

Thanks, too, to both Fr. Jim Picton and Dr. Dennis Smith, my friends and colleagues, for their unwavering support and friendship over the years through the many transitions in my life. Thanks to the readers of my newspaper columns for their letters of support and appreciation and their requests to have my articles be compiled into a book. Without their suggestions, this book may never have happened. There are numerous others I wish to thank. Thank you—One and All!

# I

# Happy New Year!

As we begin a New Year and are inching ever closer to a new century, perhaps it's a good time to take stock of our lives and what's going on in them.

Maybe we need to do more than just make the usual New Year's resolutions that we tend to forget by the end of the first month! Maybe we should look at the overall picture and ask ourselves—

What's the purpose of my life? Am I doing what I should be doing? What should I be accomplishing? Who am I? Where am I going? These questions and others which may be romping through our heads (especially at the beginning of a New Year) can become rather overwhelming and mind-boggling. How can we ever figure it all out and come to any reasonable, acceptable conclusions? The answers to these questions may be much simpler than you think.

Consider the following:

**1) To be the best person I can be**

**2) To make the world a better place because I've been here**

Both of these may imply long-term fundamental life changes rather than short-term New Year's resolutions. "To be the best person I can be" means to start right where I am. How can I improve myself physically, mentally and spiritually without being too self-critical and overly analytical? I need to accept myself where I am at this present moment and move forward from this point.

In order "To be the best person I can be" I need to be attentive, to exercise and nourish all parts of my being—the physical, emotional, mental and spiritual.

**I need to—**

**Exercise and nourish my body.** Feed it well, give it rest, relaxation, recreation, plenty of physical activity and adequate sleep and tend to all its medical needs.

**Exercise and nourish my mind.** Stretch and expand it—learn something new every day. Feed it with positive thoughts and creative mental imagery; perhaps shut off the "boob tube" or at least watch more educational, historical, or thought-provoking programs; read, study, and read some more.

**Exercise and nourish my emotions.** Recognize that all feelings are valid and learn to express them appropriately.

**Exercise and nourish my spirit.** Get acquainted with my own "Higher Self." Examine my real values and my belief systems, and reflect on whether I live out those values in daily life. Feed my spiritual self; set time aside every day for solitude, for mediation and for prayer. Read spiritual, inspirational or religious literature; attend religious services.

"To make the world a better place because I've been here" requires some deliberate intent and action. We need to be attentive to our environment and the "climate" we create around ourselves, at home, at work—or wherever we are at any moment. In fact, the present moment is all we ever really have. We can make the world a better place for ourselves and others —right here and now, this instant. One of my favorite Christ-

mas gifts is a poster with a poem by Helen Mallicoat which I
have framed and hanging on my wall as a daily reminder:

I was regretting the past
and fearing the future
Suddenly my Lord was speaking
"MY NAME IS I AM."
He paused,
I waited, He continued,
When you live in the past
with its mistakes and regrets
it is hard, I am not there
My Name is not "I Was."
When you live in the future
with its problems and fears
It is hard, I am not there
My Name is not "I WILL BE."
When you live in this moment
It is not hard, I am here
MY NAME IS I AM

In order to make the world a better place, we need to
live fully in the present moment to the best of our ability for
that is the only time we ever really have. If we can manage
that, the rest will take care of itself. We must become obser-
vant and aware in order to become able to discern what
needs to happen or change today—right now, for all of us—
you and me!

After identifying what that might be, we should ask
ourselves what we can do personally to ensure that the change
occurs. It's so easy to complain and say, "Why doesn't somebody do something?" That somebody might just be us—you
and me. If we all would do our part, the world would change in
a heartbeat!

**May your New Year be one of many happy,
growth-filled, continuous present moments.**

# 2

# You Are What You Believe

*As you think, so you are.*

We all hold deeply ingrained beliefs—about God, about ourselves, our families, our community and the world. We hold them, not necessarily because they are true—but because we believe they are true.

Our belief systems are based on our own past experiences, personal as well as global: beliefs about ourselves and our self worth, beliefs about history, beliefs about what the future may hold, beliefs about what has value and what has not.

How do we ever really know anything as factual? In the days of Columbus, it was generally believed that if you set sail on a ship and voyaged out too far, you'd fall off the face of the earth. Everyone "knew" the earth was flat. Not too many people dared to venture far from their shores. They acted on their belief system.

Our lives are profoundly influenced by what we believe, both consciously and subconsciously. Most often we are swayed much more by what we believe subconsciously than consciously, even though we actually operate out of both systems.

The conscious mind is our ordinary waking consciousness. With it we make our plans and our decisions, do our rational thinking and problem-solving. It is more or less under the control of the will.

The subconscious mind controls our breathing, digestion, circulatory system and other bodily functions over which we have little if any voluntary control. This part of us carries out all the necessary bodily functions in order to sustain life without our having to be consciously aware of it. This aspect of mind also maintains our basic habits, such as driving a car, walking and our other habitual, automatic behaviors. What a drag it would be if we had to consciously remember every step needed to get into and operate a car! Once something is learned and becomes habitual, the subconscious mind remembers, takes over and we no longer have to think about it—we just do it.

However, the subconscious mind has many other vitally important functions. It stores all memories, even pre-natal impressions. It records all thoughts, beliefs, feelings and experiences. Everything that has ever happened to us or that we have ever done, is filed away in this memory bank.

Our interpretation and perceptions of these memories and experiences are the basis of our belief systems. Some perceptions are held in the conscious mind, while others our filed away in the memory banks of our subconscious minds. Yet, filing them away out of the light of day does not eliminate them. They just go underground—especially if they are something we'd rather not remember, or something we want to hide from ourselves or from others. Out of sight is not out of mind!

The subconscious mind is analogous to a computer. What we key into it is what we pull up on our screen of life. Or, it can be compared to a garden. Whatever seeds we plant grow and become manifest in our lives.

Sometimes what we consciously think we believe is not what we really believe on a deeper level. This causes contradictions between our conscious external belief system and our subconscious internal belief system, creating all kinds of havoc in our lives. Our behavior contradicts our words. We say one thing and mean another. We become confused, depressed, anxious and angry.

In order to compensate, many of us turn to food, drugs, alcohol, promiscuity, violence. We may try to compensate with overwork because we don't know how else to cope with our frustrations—and we're sure that if we keep busy enough we won't have time to think about anything else that matters. Soon we begin to believe we are inferior, inadequate or, at best, mediocre.

What we believe determines the quality of our lives. We tend to act out and become what we believe and so create a reality for ourselves, based on our belief system. Is there anything we can do, if we don't like the reality we've created? Can we change it? You bet!

Change our belief system! To use the computer and garden analogies again: we can reprogram the computer or plant a new garden. It is with thought that we can reprogram the computer or design a new garden. Thoughts are the seeds we plant, and it is with conscious, deliberate thought that we can generate changes in our lives. Thought creates something new in the same way a seed does: it contains within itself the exact pattern of what will grow and develop. "The seeds of today become the flowers and fruits of tomorrow."

As we think about and work with the conscious and subconscious minds, we might find it a bit confusing thinking about them as two different minds. They are one and the same mind, equal in importance, just different aspects of it. One is not dominant over the other, yet they are decidedly different, each having its own unique sphere of operation. The conscious mind is assertive, directive and objective; the subconscious mind is passive, receptive and subjective. Neither is superior over the other. It is not the function of the conscious mind to be the tyrant or dictator, nor is it the function of the subconscious mind to take over and run rampant with over-wrought emotions. Each aspect of mind must be free to carry out its own particular activities, and they need to be able to work together in harmony for optimum health—physically, mentally and spiritually.

As we examine our belief systems, investigate the origin of what we believe, consciously or unconsciously we can decide whether it is still relevant to who we are today or desire to become, combine it with our own life experiences and what we wish to have manifest in our lives, we will begin to move toward a new belief system.

***And, as we believe, so shall we become.***

# 3

# The Tools of the Conscious Mind

*Whatever we can conceive and believe we can achieve.*

We all have limitless creative potential, but for many of us it is blocked, either by a lifetime of negative conditioning or by a self-limiting belief system.

This conditioning and our belief system create the reality we live in. If that reality no longer fits us, we can change it, and the agent of this change is the conscious mind.

The conscious mind is our ordinary, thinking consciousness that works with and directs the subconscious mind. Together their potential for creativity is almost limitless. Compare the mind, for a moment, to a car in your driveway with a powerful engine. The engine (the subconscious mind) has the ability and capacity to take you anywhere with great speed. But, unless you (the conscious mind) get in, turn on the ignition and get it moving, it will just sit there, rust, and never leave the driveway. So it is with the potential power of our minds.

With the conscious mind we conceive new ideas; it is also with the conscious mind that we work to achieve them. But the motive power—or engine, if you will—is belief. Unless we firmly believe in the potential, we begin to sabotage ourselves with, "Yes but" or "If only," and our ideas never come to fruition.

We have fantastic tools at our disposal through the conscious mind—tools that can truly work magic in our lives. However, even the best tools in the world need someone who knows how to use them. Becoming skilled in the use of these tools will enable us to bring about changes undreamed of. They are tools we already possess to some degree, but they need to be brought into conscious awareness and polished up a bit. These tools are observation, imagination, attention and action.

## Observation

To observe means to take notice, to become aware and to really look at the conditions of our lives. To take note of our environment, our relationships, finances, physical and emotional health, and spiritual development. It means to look beneath and beyond mere surface appearances, to look into them not just at them. Observe and take note of the things which need to change and those which can remain as they are. Whatever the conditions are, we created them—and we can change them.

## Imagination

After the observations are made and the desired changes decided upon, we need to allow the imagination to roam. The imagination is the act of forming mental pictures of something not yet actually present or experienced—creative new images.

Think big! In your mind's eye, see the desired changes as already accomplished. When the mental images, as vivid and as specific as possible, are coupled with strong feelings, the potential creativity becomes a powerful force.

## Attention

Once we've observed what we'd like changed or accomplished and have imagined what it would be like, we need to be alert and attentive. Attention extends or expands the power of observation. The dictionary defines attention as "the ability to take heed or observe carefully." Attention is the most critical and the most important of the conscious mind's tools, for without its use our desires will never see the light of day. They will remain figments of our imagination in the world of idle daydreams.

It's with alert attention that we begin to make definite plans on how to work things out. We need to be attentive to detail, using clear and specific blueprints or action plans.

## Action

When our homework is done—when we've made our observations, imagined the outcome, and attentively planned our strategies—it is time to act, to go out and do something, to follow through. We can't just sit and wait for things to fall into our laps or we might have a very long wait!

We can make the observation that have we a gift and aptitude for music, imagine giving concerts in Carnegie Hall, even buy a baby grand. But if we don't sit at that piano and practice, the baby grand will never produce our music.

The conscious mind is the transformer of life. Through the use of these tools, energy and forces are put into motion that brings about the desired change. As the imagination goes to work, mental images are planted deep in the subconscious mind, which immediately begins the process of manifestation—bringing our desires to reality.

> *To be conscious that we are perceiving or thinking is to be conscious of our own existence.*
> —Aristotle

4

# The Power of the Subconscious Mind

The human mind is indeed awesome! There hasn't been a scientific instrument devised that can equal it, even with all of our present-day sophisticated knowledge.

It has limitless potential and possibilities for creativity and further development. The conscious mind is the thinking, creative, willful part of the mind—the ordinary consciousness. We assume that most of our life's work is accomplished through the use of the conscious mind. However, the conscious mind handles only a fraction of the total mind's activity; most of it is carried out in the depth of the subconscious mind.

This aspect of the mind has been compared to an iceberg, with only a tiny portion of its tremendous bulk visible above the water. The rest is submerged and unseen. The subconscious mind automatically takes care of the vital functions of the physical body without orders from the conscious mind. But in all other matters it acts only under orders. It is sometimes called the "subjective mind" because it is "subject" to the conscious mind. However, it is in no way limited or restricted, except by the limitations placed on it by our fearful, thinking consciousness. All of us have dreamed of talents and abilities waiting to be called forth by conscious thought and desire.

The wise men of old used to tell stories and parables to help people understand abstract concepts such as that of the subconscious mind. One of these was the story of "Aladdin and His Lamp," which was used to illustrate the power of thought. As the story goes, Aladdin was given an old brass lamp. It was just an ordinary lamp like those used every day in most households—nothing special or unusual about it. It was quite by accident that the boy discovered the secret of the lamp. Whenever he rubbed it a Genie would appear to do whatever he asked.

The wise men compared the lamp to the conscious mind, just an ordinary object used every day. So ordinary, in fact, that almost no thought is given to it at all. It is totally taken for granted.

Before Aladdin could have use of his lamp he had to become aware of its tremendous power. The Genie in the lamp was in no way concerned about right or wrong, good or evil. It just did whatever was asked of it. This was a very powerful Genie and could do anything, but it had to be told exactly, in very specific terms, what was demanded, for it would bring exactly what was requested. Sometimes what Aladdin got was not what he meant, but it was always what he asked for. What he asked for, he got.

So it is with the subconscious mind, the Genie within each of us. It brings what we ask for, not always what we thought we asked for! It works with clear images and visualizations coupled with strong feelings. The clearer the image, the stronger the feeling and the more powerful the Genie.

Why aren't there more geniuses like Beethoven, Mozart, Einstein, and Edison in all our families if we all have a powerful Genie at our beck and call? It's because most of us are unaware. We have to "know" before we can "rub the lamp." We hold deeply ingrained beliefs about our potential or limitations. What we believe, we act upon. "What we think about, we bring about."

We program the subconscious mind through our belief systems, thoughts and desires. The subconscious then interprets that as something we want more of. So it does just that—it brings us more of the same. Our thoughts, habits and characteristic ways of responding to persons, places or events determine the quality of our lives. If there are things in our lives we'd like to add, change or "delete" in order to enhance or improve the quality of life for ourselves and for those around us, we can do that.

The way to do that is with the "tools of the conscious mind" (see Chapter 3) to change our thought patterns and habits. Our habitual thought patterns and habits sometimes are difficult to change. The subconscious mind may rebel and resist these changes at first, especially if they've held reign for a long time, but it is subject to the conscious mind. It can and will comply.

*Change a thought and you change an act,*

*Change an act and you change a habit.*

*Change a habit, and you change a character*

*Change a character and you change a destiny.*

—Author unknown

5

# The Importance of Positive Self-Esteem

Our whole quality of life depends on our estimation
of ourselves, for what we believe about ourselves,
we project to others and to the world at large.

The most valuable gift we can bestow on family, friends
and our community is our own personal sense of self-worth.
Feeling good about oneself rubs off on others and enhances
their own sense of self-worth. Appreciating our own gifts and
talents frees us to share them with others, encourages them to
try their own wings, to the advantage of everyone.

We've heard it said many times that charity begins at
home. Where is our closest "home" if it isn't within our very
own self? The word, "charity" implies love and care. Self-love
does not indicate that one is self-centered, self-seeking, selfish,
greedy, conceited or egotistic. Rather, it denotes self-respect,
confidence, self-reliance, independence and a sense of pride in
one's own being.

The fear of being labeled as "selfish" inhibits us all at
times, and interferes with our ability to take care of ourselves

and our own needs. In our concern over this label, we are often guilty of the most gross self-neglect. Self-care and self-preservation is a primary obligation and responsibility.

The word, "duty" seems to apply only to our obligation to others, to be "good to the very last drop" until we drop, depleted, exhausted, and worse yet, even unappreciated for all our efforts. Yet, our first duty is to ourselves. The commandment to "Love thy neighbor as thyself" can mean nothing to us—if we don't begin with "thyself."

How can we care for others if we ourselves are needy? How can we create happiness in our homes and communities if we ourselves are miserable and unhappy? We can't love anyone or anything unless we esteem or value them highly. If we believe in our hearts that we are untrustworthy, we cannot trust others. If we have no self-respect, we don't respect others. If we feel we are unworthy or unlovable we are unable to love others. Whether we are aware of it or not, we externalize our inner feelings about ourselves and cast them out onto others.

We can't give something we don't have. So often we run around with an empty cup and try to give from that drained mug. We must first of all keep our own cup full—give of the overflowing to others, but keep ours full. Only then can we give freely and share the wonderful gift of self. Only then can we help others keep their cups full as well. To be able to give and receive, we must have something to give and we can't do that from an empty, drained cup.

How can we fill our cups and keep them full? Heed our own needs. Define what those needs are and attend to them. We must take time to listen, really listen to ourselves as we ask ourselves some questions such as—

    **1) How can I nurture myself without taking from others?**

    **2) Do I carry burdens that others should carry themselves?**

3) Do I accept or assume blame too readily?

4) Do I allow others to rule my thinking?

5) Do I give myself permission to relax, rest and enjoy myself?

6) Do I believe that self-care means self-indulgence?

7) Do I attend to my health, nutrition and exercise needs?

8) Am I aware and attend to my psychological and spiritual needs?

9) How do I define happiness and well-being?

10) Do I consider myself a valuable, worthwhile human being?

Taking the time to reflect on these questions, and write out our thoughts and answers—as well as other questions that may arise—and then to make the necessary changes should help to fill our cups. And we'll begin to realize the vital importance of good self-care and positive self-esteem.

Why is it so important? Because positive self-esteem is the basic ingredient for happiness, and a crucial component in mental health: it is indispensable for parents to be able to bequeath the gift of a good self-esteem to their children. Above all, it is essential for a faith-filled spiritual life.

Love is the greatest gift we can bestow to loved ones and to the world, and love is born out of good self-esteem and a sense of self-worth.

*This above all: to thine own self be true*
*And it must follow, as night the day*
*Thou canst not then be false to any man.*

*Hamlet, William Shakespeare*

## 6

# I Can Do Anything Just for Today

Sometimes we become so overwhelmed worrying about what happened in the past and what might happen in the future, that we lose sight of the present today.

There really isn't much we can do about the past or the future. The past is gone, behind us, and the future isn't here yet. AH, but there is TODAY! We can decide what *today* will be like.

This is the first day of the rest of your life. What will you do with it? If you knew this was the last day of your life, what would you do with it? Today is it! Today is all you have! Let's not waste anymore of our todays worrying about yesterday or tomorrow.

**JUST FOR TODAY** I will be happy. "Most folks are as happy as they make up their minds to be." (Abe Lincoln) Put on a happy face, make up your mind that today's a good day, and it will be.

**JUST FOR TODAY** I won't worry about tomorrow. Tomorrow can take care of itself. When tomorrow becomes today-then is the time to tackle its issues.

**JUST FOR TODAY** I will look for and appreciate the beauty around me. I will look as attractive as I can, myself; I will see the beauty in others; I will appreciate and enjoy the colors, sounds and the beauty of nature.

**JUST FOR TODAY** I will take good care of my health. I will eat only nutritious food, drink plenty of water, get some exercise and take time for rest and relaxation.

**JUST FOR TODAY** I will stimulate my mind. I will exercise my brain cells by reading or studying something which requires some effort and concentration.

**JUST FOR TODAY** I will strengthen my spiritual life through prayer meditation, music, read scripture or other inspiring, uplifting literature. I will give thanks for all the good in my life.

**JUST FOR TODAY** I will express love in every way I can, with family and loved ones, with friends and co-workers, with anyone I meet today—with a smile, a kind word, a thoughtful act.

We can do anything—one day at time. Then soon our many one-day-at-a-time's become a way of life, a habitual way of being and behaving. And much to our surprise, one day we'll wake up to find life is so much fuller, so much happier than we ever dreamed was possible!

# 7

# What Is Unconditional Love?

Love is a decision, not a feeling. Choosing to love is really choosing a way of life—a way to respond to others and life's events rather than just reacting to them.

The decisions or choices we make influence our thoughts and our behavior; our thoughts and behavior influence our feelings. "Thought fuels feelings and feelings fuel thoughts," and together they may bring about those deep, wonderful emotions we call love. We love because we decide to.

We've been told that we should love unconditionally. But what does that mean? Does it mean that we should think only of the "other"— his or her needs and desires to the detriment of our own? Sometimes! Sometimes yes—and sometimes no. It may be difficult at times to know where unconditional love ends and co-dependency begins.

Perhaps the best lived-out definition of unconditional love is that of a parent for a newborn. We don't say, "I'll love you if you won't wake me up at two in the morning crying and wanting to be fed." Or, "I'll love you if you don't soil your diapers umpteen times a day." It's expected, it's a given: we lovingly do what needs to be done. So what, if we're tired and can't catch up on our sleep? So what if the crying gets on our nerves? That's one form of unconditional love and total acceptance.

That kind of unconditional love and acceptance pertains to self as well as to others, however. It's not an either-or choice. It includes putting a value on ourselves and our needs. It also includes some difficult things at times such as discipline, pain, loss, separation. It includes rather wonderful, beautiful things at times—such as mutual support, friendship, companionship, sexual intimacy, help in time of crisis and continual growth together in love.

Love and commitment are decisions, not feelings, and as such involve the act of the will, which in turn may involve self-denial or the denial of the wishes of another. Unconditional love is not all sweetness and light, cuddling or coddling. It may at times need to become "tough love." It may mean that restrictions be put on the behavior of a rebellious teenager; insistence that not another drink be consumed by an already inebriated spouse; or the placement of an elderly loved one in a nursing home for the best possible care. Love is not for sissies or the faint-hearted. It can be very hard work.

We all have a deep need to belong—to be a part of someone's life—which can have both healthy and unhealthy components. To many, unconditional love really means ownership or possession of another person's body, mind and soul. This is not love but bondage. I love the writings of Kahil Kibran; following is an excerpt from his book, *The Prophet*, on the subject of love and marriage.

*Love one another but make not a bond of love:*
*Let it rather be a moving sea between the shores of*
*your soul.*
*Fill each other's cup but drink not from one cup.*
*Give one another of your bread but eat not from the*
*same loaf.*
*And stand together yet not too near together:*
*for the pillar and the temple stand apart.*
*And the oak tree and the cypress grow not in each*
*other's shadow.*

Though in the above quote Kibran is addressing marital love primarily, this is a description of how love should be lived out in all areas of life—between parents and children, siblings, friends, and so on.

One of the fundamental gifts of unconditional love is the freedom to be yourself. With someone we truly love and who loves us, each of us feels free to express thoughts and feelings with confidence—even to disagree without fear of rejection.

This freedom empowers one to become his or her own person, to develop the potential gifts and talents each of us possess in order to become who we were created to be. Love makes the world go round. It makes dreary days brighter, brings light into the eyes and new life to the world, puts a smile on the lips and a song in the heart. "Love is a many splendored thing."

To love unconditionally and to be loved unconditionally is a reflection of God's love for all of His creation. It is what eternally creates and sustains the Universe.

*Someday after we have mastered the winds, the waves, the gravity, we will harness for God the energies of Love, and then for the second time in the history of the world, man will have discovered fire.*

—Tielhard de Chardin S.J.

## 8

# Healthy Shame or Unhealthy Shame

We all experience feelings of shame now and then; it's a normal part of the human condition.

Just what is shame? The dictionary defines it as "an emotion caused by the consciousness of something wrong in one's conduct or state (of being); a cause of disgrace." Sometimes the emotion of shame is a healthy, normal response to a given situation. At other times, it can become pathological and unhealthy causing a great deal of mental, emotional pain and anguish.

I'll share a little story with you as an illustration. A number of years ago, I went on a European tour with some friends. Three of us decided to try a little restaurant in Rome. They were serving a smorgasbord as well as single entrees, and I chose the smorgasbord. Now, when you eat at a smorgasbord, you put a little of everything you want on your plate. Right? Wrong! "When in Rome, do as the Romans do." Well, not being Roman and not knowing what Romans do (put each item on its own little dish) I put a little bit of this and a little bit of that on my plate, then perched a piece of pie on top of it and walked blithely to my table completely oblivious to stares aimed at me.

The first inkling I had that something was amiss, was when a horrified waiter came bearing down on me saying, "No, no, NO! Madam!" and took the pie off my plate placed it on its own dish over on the edge of the table. I looked around and everyone in the place was staring at me. I felt I could read their minds. "Look at that vulgar American, eating like a pig at a trough!"

And what were my "loyal, true-blue" friends (who'd ordered single entrees) doing during my public disgrace? They just sat there, eyes downcast, hand clasped, lips tightly pursed so they wouldn't burst into wild laughter—and let me suffer my shame, disgrace and embarrassment all by myself. I was wishing that the floor would open up and swallow me. At that point, I couldn't even eat. I even felt a brief flash of rage at my friends. I don't know what I expected them to do—at least they stayed with me, and didn't act as though they didn't even know me!

The point is that as intense as my feelings of shame and embarrassment were, they were normal, healthy, and only temporary. It might have degenerated into an unhealthy shame if I'd allowed that one experience to ruin my whole trip—if I'd defined myself as an uncouth, vulgar pig, even though I may have acted like one and others may have perceived me as such. Once outside the restaurant, we dissolved into howls of laughter.

Healthy shame is just as intense and unpleasant as unhealthy shame, with the difference that we can recover from it sooner. It is only temporary, but it can have a lasting impact. (I'll never do that again, if I ever go back to Rome). It does tend to keep one humble and helps one to realize that we are all in the wonderful boat of humanity together.

We all make mistakes and make fools of ourselves at times. We suffer deep chagrin, loss of face and would do anything to have it not have happened.

But it's like the spoken word. Once it's out there, it's out there—nothing you can do will unsay or undo it. Shame can become unhealthy and toxic in our lives if it becomes a constant companion. Unhealthy shame doesn't admit that we have flaws and make mistakes. It says we are flaws and our whole lives are mistakes.

Our long-term response to humiliating events, our feelings and reactions, determine our emotional health regarding shame. You can admit you've made a fool of yourself, or behaved like an idiot and still be OK. It's when you carry it further and say (and believe), "I am a fool or an idiot" that you find yourself bound up by unhealthy shame.

Some symptoms of unhealthy shame include a) chronic low self-esteem, b) fear of self-exposure, keeping most of your life a secret, c) continual self blame and self criticism; d) relationships with people who don't value you, listen to you or take you seriously.

There are some steps you can take which may help "heal the shame that binds you" (Title of a book by John Bradshaw) such as:

> **Stop the self blame.** Don't allow words and thoughts such as "crazy, stupid, fat, dumb, ugly" to go roaming around in your head. Stop! Give yourself permission to be less than perfect.

> **Share your story,** confide in a friend. You may be surprised to learn that many people have had similar experiences—you are not alone.

**Act as if you are a happy, confident, self-respecting person,** and soon you will be. To "act as if" may seem like a game of pretend at first, but it works.

**Give yourself time.** Your feeling and attitudes may have been with you since childhood—they won't be rooted out overnight, but they can and will change.

**Surround yourself with people** you can relax with, share your stories with and just be yourself. Choose friends carefully.

Set time aside to be with that wonderful person—YOU! Take time for rest and solitude, for exercise, for mini-vacations by yourself. Walk on the beach or along a river, spend an afternoon with a good book, make a prayerful visit to a church or chapel. Take time to be good to yourself and heal.

*You are a Child of the Universe—you have a right to be here.*

—Desiderata

# 9

# Moving Beyond Codependency

Codependence is sometimes confused with unconditional love. The assumption is that with unconditional love you give your "all"—all you've got—anything less is not enough.

There is the same assumption with codependence—that the welfare of others is totally your responsibility. What does the term, "codependence" mean? It has been defined over and over by many different professionals working in the field, but we still don't have a standard definition. John Bradshaw's explanation is simple and to the point: "A lack or loss of self-identity."

Persons who lack self-identity place little or no value on the self, don't know who they are and don't think it matters. All that matters is what other people think and feel and what their needs are. These people often become compulsive about everything and become workaholics, obsessive caretakers, volunteering for everything that comes along. They run around from dawn to dusk "doing good" until they drop from sheer exhaustion and utter frustration. Whatever they do—no matter how hard they try—it is never enough! They suffer terribly from the "if only's." "If only I hadn't said that, maybe he wouldn't have gone out and gotten drunk, or maybe she wouldn't have had an accident, or maybe he wouldn't have become ill. If only I'd tried harder to please. It's my fault. Everything is always my fault. I can never do things right!"

The sad part of it all is—it's true! We can't ever do it all and we can't always do it right. We can't ever please all the people in our lives all of the time. Even if we had somehow taken care of all the "if only's" we knew about, others would emerge we didn't know about. It's like pouring sand down a rat hole—a bottomless pit we can never fill.

This is not to say that it's abnormal to feel dependent at times, and for others to be dependent on us. We all go through times when we need others to be there for us. Sometimes this is normal and healthy, other times it is not.

Then we may experience times of independence. Like the two-year-old who shouts, "No! me do it," we may scorn help and assistance even when needed. Again, sometimes this is normal and healthy; other times it is not.

Those who never validate their own feelings or opinions, who rarely make decisions for fear of making mistakes and who rely totally on others for their sense of self-worth, suffer from an unhealthy dependence.

Those who don't place any value whatever on others' feelings and opinions; who always put their own feelings and desires first; who believe they don't need anybody are on the other end of an unhealthy dependence-to-independence spectrum.

The truth is we are all "inter-dependent." We all need each other and are needed by others at different times for different reasons. Interdependence means that sometimes we give and sometimes we take. Sometimes we may need healing, sometimes we may be the healer. We can never be all things to another, neither can we be totally self-sufficient.

Inter-dependence creates harmonious balance. When our relationships are harmonious and balanced, we feel more secure even in times of insecurity. We can disagree without the world falling apart.

We can say, "No," without feeling guilty and we can say, "Yes," readily and generously. We can take risks more freely; can make decisions more readily and assume the responsibility for our own happiness.

Through developing inter-dependent relationships, we begin to accept, understand and be responsible for our own feelings and desires and permit others to do the same. We are not held accountable for the happiness of others nor are they for ours. If we can become answerable for our own lives, become happy, productive, fun-loving and spiritually fulfilled ourselves—it rubs off—thus encouraging and enabling others to do likewise.

The lack of self-identity so disabling in the codependent state is gradually transformed into a healthy self-esteem as we take our first faltering steps towards interdependence. It ends the fear of dependent codependence of never being good enough or of being able to make it alone. It also ends the fear of having to go it alone with the "stiff-upper lip" of rugged independence. Interdependence means we're in it together for the long haul with mutual support and love.

***"No man is an island"***

—John Dunn

*Teach me to feel another's woe,*

*to hide the fault I see;*

*That mercy that I to others show*

*That mercy show to me.*

—Alexander Pope, "The Universal Prayer"

# 10

# What Forgiveness Is—
# and Isn't

When clients come into my office suffering from a world of hurt, they are often holding on to deep emotional wounds, either self-inflicted or caused by others, along with feelings of guilt, remorse, grief, despair, depression and so on.

Expressions such as, "I just can't handle this," "How do I ever get over this?" "I'll never be able to trust anyone ever again!" "I don't know what to do!" "I need help," poignantly verbalize the distress they are suffering.

Healing such deep wounds cannot happen as long as we hang on to them. We must forgive and let go. At times I would get reactions such as "Forgive? Never!" "It's too awful, I just don't think that I can," or, "If I do, it implies that it was OK—and it wasn't!" Another may simply say, "No! I don't ever want to forgive that so-and-so." Such feelings are normal, human reactions to being hurt and are perfectly understandable.

Yet, understandable as these emotions are, they aren't helpful to either our health or our happiness. How can we forgive if we don't really feel like it—especially when we believe our feelings of outrage are justified? The answer is to acknowledge our feelings. They are valid. Consider the consequences of hanging on to them: grudges, resentments, anxiety, hatred, and negative thought patterns all build up and bring on more pain and loss. "Acid only harms the container it's in!" We have to decide whether we want to remain stuck where we are or let go and move on.

We always have choices. We can choose to remain where we are, keep on hurting, and plot revenge—or we can choose to heal ourselves through forgiveness and build a new life. Forgiveness is a vital first step toward healing and toward wholeness—a step that will totally change our quality of life.

Like any major step we take in life, it is a volitional one. That is, it's an act of the will—it doesn't just happen. Forgiveness is a decision, not a feeling. All feelings to the contrary, we'll forgive when we decide to. When we do decide to, we will change our thoughts, words and actions accordingly. Change these and our feelings will follow suit.

Forgiveness does not imply condoning wrongful, hurtful acts against us. It doesn't mean that people should not be held accountable for their transgressions or that we allow ourselves to become victims, doormats or laid-back marshmallows! What it does imply is to "Wash those hurts right out of your hair," and allow them to slide back into the past. We can't change the past, but we can change our present by how we react to the past—in the here and now.

Real forgiveness is not sentimental, it's not condescending, and above all it is not conditional. "I'll forgive you if—" or "I'll forgive you when—." It isn't even necessary to tell people we've forgiven them; it's enough to do so in our own minds and hearts.

Forgiveness is a way of life—a kind of readiness to let go of the little everyday hurts and annoyances that are part and parcel of life.

This kind of readiness prepares us for any major hurts that may come our way. It means accepting people as they are—without judgment. It means taking risks, making us vulnerable to being hurt again. But it also strengthens us and our trust in ourselves to be able to cope with anything and not be bowled over.

The most difficult person to forgive is often ourselves, for we are frequently harder on ourselves than we are on anyone else. To candidly look at our own failings, mistakes, faults and transgressions can be most difficult. But self-recrimination and self-loathing are self-defeating. The decision to forgive applies to self as well as to others. We need to turn our attention to what we can do to make amends or restitution for any wrongs we may have committed, take care of it, let go and move on.

Forgiveness is to choose love rather than bitterness and hatred.

It is looking forward not backward. This choice is a way of life that frees the forgiver. Healing begins when we free ourselves to love and accept ourselves and others. To be healed is to be made whole. To be made whole is to be made holy. Let healing begin.

*To err is human, to forgive divine*

—Alexander Pope

*God asks not for our ability*

*or our inability,*

*but for our availability*

—Anonymous

# 11

# The Journey from Ashes to Easter

Lent is a period of forty days beginning on Ash Wednesday and ending on Easter Sunday. It is a time set aside by Christians the world over as a time for reflection: a time to look at and question our assumptions about life, the meaning of life, and our spirituality.

These six and a half weeks can be an enriching spiritual journey or an "interior process" of conversion, repentance, prayer and spiritual growth.

Spirituality and spiritual growth mean different things to different people. To some it may mean getting more intimately involved with the church of their choice. To those who are not church-affiliated, it may mean getting in touch with their own mortality, and growing closer to God or the Supreme Being. It may mean taking more time for prayer and meditation and getting in touch with the Higher Self—the God within.

Traditionally, Lent is a time to make small "sacrifices"—to give up something or to do something out of the ordinary to keep this special time in mind—to remind us to stop, reflect on what life is all about and what we can do to enhance the meaning of life for ourselves and everyone we connect with. What should I give up for Lent? Whatever stands in my way of my inner journey toward spiritual renewal.

It may be something as simple as turning off the TV and reading something inspiring or spiritually uplifting. It may mean some real behavioral changes—becoming more thoughtful of others, giving up excuses for doing or not doing something—returned kindness for rudeness—going the "extra mile." It may mean refraining from the use of alcohol or drugs; eating less—fasting; making contributions to food banks and charities. It may mean giving up the preoccupation with the self and becoming more involved with others—being nice to someone you don't like. The list could go on and on. If we really look within, we know what areas of life we need to improve. Taking the time this "interior process" requires for the six and a half weeks of Lent could change the quality of our entire lives.

It is also a time to reflect on what our beliefs are regarding life after death. Do we believe in a "resurrection?" If so, how does our belief affect the way we live out our lives? Ash Wednesday gets us in touch with our physical mortality. Easter Sunday gets us in touch with our spiritual immortality. Many Christian churches have the tradition of tracing with ashes a small cross on a person's forehead as a symbol of our fragile mortality, our need for repentance for wrongdoing, and our need for conversion to a new and better way of life and a more intimate relationship with God.

As we travel on this journey from the "Ashes" of the old self to the "Easter" of the new self, may we discard old negative habits and take on more positive life-giving ones. We may then experience our own "rising from the ashes" as we celebrate the spiritual renewal of Easter.

*Dust thou art, to dust returnest, was not spoken to the Soul.*

—Henry Wadsworth Longfellow

# 12

# Keep the Candles of Your Marriage Lit

A happy, successful marriage can be compared to a candelabra or "wedding candle" holding three candles lit and burning brightly with two smaller candles on either side of a large middle candle.

They are part of one unit with three separate components. The smaller candles represent the bride and groom and the larger center candle symbolizes their marriage relationship.

A happy marriage is a delicate balancing act of keeping all three candles lit—together yet apart, functioning individually and as a unit. "To sing and dance together and be joyous but let each be alone—even as the strings of a lute are alone though they quiver with the same music." (*The Prophet*—Kahill Gibran).

How to stand together, yet apart; how to become One yet remain separate is no easy task. Witness the high divorce rates! If a couple exists only for each other they become too dependent and enmeshed. There isn't enough room to breathe; they smother each other and soon one or both of the smaller candles goes out for lack of air or space.

If a couple is bent on each doing his or her "own thing," they become too independent. There's too much room and air between them; there's a strong "draft" and the middle candle blows out—even though the individual candles may remain lit.

The secret to keeping all three candles lit is to strike a happy medium of being neither too dependent on each other nor too independent of each other. We can call this state "interdependence."

The prefix, "inter-" means, "mutual, reciprocal, or between." Interdependence, then, means a mutual give-and-take, a being there for each other in the good, the bad or the in-between times. Yet, at the same time, each takes full responsibility for his or her own growth, well-being and happiness. All this is so much easier said than done! We can't just lump all marriages into one basket and say, "If you do thus and so, you'll live 'happily ever after.'" Not so! Each marriage is as unique and different as each individual in the relationship. What may work for one marriage may lead another straight to the divorce court.

It may take some time and discernment to come to the place of interdependence for each unique relationship. However, here are some general guidelines that may apply to all:

**Be yourself, your own person—and allow your mate the same privilege and opportunity.**

**Never expect another to make you happy.**

**Never accept responsibility for another's happiness.**

**Have realistic expectations. No one person can ever be all things to another.**

**Keep romance alive.**

**Renew your commitment to each other from time to time.**

**Have fun and enjoy each other; also spend time alone.**

**Be attentive to the spiritual aspects of life.**

Unity as one but individuality as persons brings the best of all worlds into the marital relationship. As Kahill Gibran says, "Stand together, yet not too close together, for the pillars in the temple, and the oak tree and the cypress grow not in each other's shadow."

***Together—yet apart. Keep those candles burning!***

# 13

# The Three Cs of Marriage

Communication, Conflict and Change are the three "C words" which may become "pebbles on the path" of any marital relationship. If they are not understood, addressed and dealt with, they may become major "stumbling stones" to trip over and cause us to fall.

These three Cs are a normal part of all the areas of everyday life, and they are especially important in marital relationships. We all need to be able to communicate well, to handle conflict with the least amount of stress and to accept the fact that change is an inevitable fact of life.

Communication is a vital factor in how the wheel of life turns—whether the road is smooth and even or rough, bumpy and downright unpleasant. It's the way we connect with others, and a deep connection makes it all worth while—especially in the marital relationship.

None of us is a "born communicator;" it is a skill we all must learn. Speaking and hearing are taken so much for granted that we pay little attention to how we carry out these important functions. Some of us are good at speaking out but never really "hear" the other. Some of us hear just fine but never express our own thoughts and feelings. And sometimes our verbal language is incongruent with our nonverbal language.

There are four basic steps to effective communication:

**1) Speak clearly.**

**2) Listen intently.**

**3) Maintain eye contact.**

**4) Be attentive to the non-verbals.**

Sounds rather simple doesn't it? Wrong! There are so many complex facets to the way we communicate that unless we are alert and aware, we may miss much of what is going on. In order to "really hear," we need to be able to listen on many levels—to be able to hear the words that are spoken as well as the nonverbal "body language." We need to become able to "read between the lines."

How do we communicate non-verbally? With every fiber of our being—with our eyes, hands, voice tone, facial expressions, tears, smiles, posture, gesture, breathing, movement, sex. Our non-verbal communications can be far more expressive than our verbal language.

The problem is that often our verbal and nonverbal languages are incongruent. They don't match up! If we tell our spouse how much we love him or her and then behave in an unloving, inconsiderate manner, which message will be believed? We must learn to say what we mean and mean what we say so each will be heard and none will be hurt.

Conflict is often very much a part of how we communicate. "Into each life some rain must fall," and you may feel like continuing the song with, "and too much is falling in mine!" Conflict is present at some time in all close relationships. It sort of "goes with the territory." We all want to protect our own turf, our own opinions, our own values. We don't want to hear the other side for fear that giving in or letting go would mean "losing."

The very word "conflict" makes some people nervous. They think of it as fighting, struggle, discord, arguments, disagreements, antagonism, hostility, violence. Yet, it is not conflict itself that matters so much as does our response to it. In times of conflict, another "C-word" may emerge—the need to "control." The desire for control or the fear of being controlled often stems from repeated win/lose situations.

If we can fine-tune our communication skills and apply them, we can learn how to compromise (another "C-word") so that both may experience winning more often. Sometimes we have to accept the fact that we may "win a few" or "lose a few." "You can't win 'em all!"

Change is another concept that is unsettling to many. The honeymoon phase won't last forever. Kids come along, illness or unemployment may strike, and we all get older. There's nothing as constant as change itself. We may all long for the "good old days," or wail, "If only things were like they used to be!" But if we really think about it, would we really want that? Without change there would be nothing new, nothing exciting around the corner. It could get boring!

Change means growth, new possibilities, and yes, some things we'd rather avoid. But it's all a part of the ongoing spiral of life. We can stand against it, try to keep things the same—but in the end we'll be blown over by the winds of change. Or we can "ride the wind" together and see where it takes us.

As we learn how to integrate the three Cs—Communication, Conflict and Change—and recognize them as a normal part of marriage, a fourth "C-word" may emerge: Contentment. And we may come closer to "living happily ever after" than we ever dreamed possible.

*There is no more lovely, friendly and charming relationship, communion or company than a good marriage.*

—Martin Luther

14

# About Quarreling

Show me two people who claim they never quarrel,
and I'll show you two people who never live out
their relationship to its fullest potential.

Disagreements and quarrels are a normal part of living and should be viewed as such. They can be very
unpleasant and cause much anguish and pain. They can be
divisive and have disastrous consequences. They can also be
a means to express one's feelings to the fullest, clear up
serious misunderstandings and become a bridge to closer
intimacy. Quarrels, brought to a healthy, healing conclusion,
can do much to help smooth out the rough edges of a relationship.

We need to be able to define the "what" of the quarrel before we can move to the "how" of the quarrel. Sometimes it is not so much the "what" of the quarrel as it is the
"how" that matters, but both need to be attended to. What is
really being said? Stop shouting and listen! So often all the
shouting is not about what we believe it is about. We may
not be upset for the reasons we think, and say we are,
because a "hidden agenda" may be lurking somewhere
beneath the surface which needs to be brought out into the

open and resolved. A quarrel is a symptom that something in the relationship needs attention—now!

Quarrels may be either an effective tool to clear the air and resolve issues or a destructive explosion. "Effective quarreling?" you may ask. This is what happens when we are able to get to the real problems or issues, resolve them and move forward. Following are some suggestions for effective quarreling:

1) **Stop and listen to the other person. Be attentive, make eye contact.**

2) **Make no assumptions that you've really heard what was said and meant. Paraphrase using words such as, "Are you saying that...?"**

3) **Take turns to respond to each other's statements. Respond (with understanding) rather than react (with hostility).**

4) **Stick to the here and now. Bring up only what's pertinent to this discussion. Do not bring up old "garbage"—reminders of past transgressions and hurts.**

5) **Suggest a compromise or alternate solution acceptable to both of you.**

6) **Call a truce if you can't seem to come to a com-**

promise. Go apart for about an hour and think. Write down the pros and cons in the argument and consider both sides honestly. Write down a possible compromise or solution you could live with.

7) Come together again and as calmly as possible, share your thoughts and ideas.

8) If there is still an impasse, "agree to disagree" for the time being, and set another time to continue the discussion.

9) As much as possible, remain calm. A quiet mind can think and reason more clearly and is much better focused.

10) Try to find some humor in the situation. Many a quarrel can be dissipated in laughter.

11) Don't end the day and go to bed in anger. If the issue isn't resolved, table it. Call a temporary truce and sleep on it. Things may look brighter tomorrow.

12) If after all of the above, things are still unresolved, don't hesitate to seek professional help. Your relationship is too precious.

Lighten up, learn to laugh at yourself and remember the "good times." Keep your mind focused on the positive. Pray for love and peace in both your hearts and ask God to be present in your relationship.

When the quarrel is behind you and issues resolved, laugh and cry, kiss and make up. A good, hearty quarrel talked through, with both sides feeling really listened to and "heard" can lead to much closer intimacy.

A healthy relationship allows partners the freedom to be themselves, to be individuals, not joined at the hip. Each can have his or her own opinions and ideas without feeling threatened. Naturally conflicts and differences can and will occur in any relationship from time to time. That's a normal part of life. However, if mutual trust, tolerance and respect have been built up these differences are acceptable. Feelings are expressed and heard by the other rather than denied or suppressed and thus the resolution of problems and difficulties becomes a normal part of life.

***To truly hear is to heal.***

## 15

# Viva la Difference

As I've listened to couples over the years, I've often observed one person staring at the other in incredulous disbelief at what was just said, as though the other had just flown in from another planet!

They seem to exist in two different worlds, the man and the woman, and, indeed, they are different. Not only are men and women different in their physical attributes, but they also think, feel and express themselves differently. Research has shown that even the brains of men and women are constructed differently.

Those who keep flying the "banners of equality" will just have to keep them flapping in the breeze. "It ain't never gonna happen!" That's not bad; in fact, it's wonderful and exciting. There's plenty of room for the wonderful qualities of both men and women.

One of the major differences is the way men and women view power. Generally speaking, women view power as "power for" and men view it as "power over."

"Power for" speaks of empowerment, gentleness, acceptance, cooperation, assertion (vs aggression). Women look for ways to connect and communicate when problems arise. Their feelings and emotions are generally involved in any given situation.

"Power over" speaks of dominance, authority, control, conquest and aggression. Men tend to bring logic, reason, control or force to their problem-solving repertoire. Their approach is often more cognitive than emotive.

Power is a neutral force, and the desire for power is a normal part of life. It's what keeps the world turning. The art of negotiation includes the ability to understand the other's viewpoint or needs, (power for) which is something women are often very good at; this is not to imply that the more masculine traits of logic, control or tenacity (power over) are not equally important. A blending of both is the ideal. Both are needed. It need not be an "either-or" choice; it can be a "both-and" situation.

Just as men and women use their power differently, their method of communication also varies. How often I've heard a client wail, "There's just no communicating! No matter how hard I try, I just can't get through!" And it's true! They are coming from different corners of the boxing ring! When women try to communicate, it is usually an attempt to make a connection or to try to understand. When men strive at communication, they are motivated more by the desire to inform in a logical way, or to fix whatever is wrong. This drives women nuts.

A woman may be feeling upset and just wants to be heard, held or understood. The man may respond with something like, "Oh come now, it isn't that bad," in an effort to lighten things up. Instead, she feels belittled, patronized, and unheard. He feels confused and bewildered, wonders what's wrong; he was only trying to help. Neither is able to get beneath the skin of the other and comprehend what's really going on between them.

It is indeed difficult to understand the opposite sex. It isn't called the "opposite sex" for nothing! And if that weren't bad enough, each of us has some of the "opposite sex" within—making it difficult to understand ourselves at times, much less the other person.

The traditional masculine qualities of logic, assertiveness, aggressiveness and more active tendencies are also present in a woman and are called her "Animus." The softer, more feminine traits such as tenderness, nurture, and more passive tendencies in a man are called his "Anima."

These are wonderful qualities we all possess, and when well balanced and understood could go a long way in helping men and women appreciate and respect each other. When a man is tenderly taking care of his child, attending to the needs of a sick wife or an elderly parent, his "Anima" is on deck. When a woman is running her company, taking care of things in an assertive, logical manner she is using her "Animus." Some men have a strongly developed Anima; some women have a powerful Animus. Both are normal and healthy—just different.

This is often misunderstood in our society, between the sexes and within ourselves. A deeply caring man is called a "wimp." An assertive capable woman is categorized as a "bitch." This is a tragic state of affairs. It can inhibit people from being or becoming who they really are and causes much needless pain and anguish.

If we can just get into our own skins, understand and appreciate the different aspects within ourselves, we might have an easier time valuing, honoring and respecting the precious uniqueness in the men and women in our lives.

There need not be a battle going on between the sexes. We can all proclaim "VIVA LA DIFFERENCE" and celebrate those differences.

*It is good to be just plain happy*
*It is a little better to know that you are happy;*
*but to understand that you are happy*
*and to know how and why and still be happy*
*be happy in the being and the knowing,*
*well, that is beyond happiness*
*that is bliss.*
　　　　　　—Henry Miller, "The Colossus of Maroussi"

# 16

# The Pursuit of Happiness

Our country's Constitution guarantees our right "to the pursuit of happiness." But alas! It doesn't tell us how or where to find it. And, looking for it in all the wrong places leads to many of our ills—physically, mentally, emotionally and spiritually.

What is this thing called "happiness?" It is difficult to come up with a blanket definition because it is such an individual "something"—such an individual state of mind. To some it means an activity-packed calendar; to others it means privacy, quiet time, or time to spend with loved ones, a place in the country, a good marriage, you name it.

Whatever it is, it is worth seeking. Happiness is a true guardian of the quality of life. It is a guardian of good mental, emotional and physical health, of family and friendships, and a guardian of peace. Yet, sometimes it seems so illusive. We think we almost have it and then, like quicksilver, it slips out of our grasp.

What are some of the causes of unhappiness? Their name is legion! One of the top-ranking ones is family instability...fighting and quarreling between husband and wife, parents and kids, between siblings; divorce or the death of a loved one. Others include job frustrations, unemployment, poverty, alcoholism, violence, illness, low self-esteem; the list is endless.

Some people seem to be "allergic" to happiness. If things seem to be going right, they don't trust it. They look for the flaws they are sure are there, wait for "the other shoe to drop," pick a fight for no good reason, create chaos where there is none. They have a tendency to accentuate the negative rather than the positive.

It isn't that happier people don't experience these same frustrations. The best of families fight at times, experience illness, and many of the other "bad things that happen to good people." It's a matter of a person's attitude and response to things that happen, not what happens. As Abraham Lincoln once said, "People are about as happy as they make up their minds to be," and, "Happiness is when our thinking is pleasant a good share of the time." When George Burns at age 95 was asked the secret of a long happy life, he said, "Fall in love with what you do for a living." Norman Vincent Peal calls it the "Plus Factor"—always seeing the cup half full rather than half empty; seeking and finding the "plus side" of things rather than the "lacking side."

Happiness is the best medicine for all the ills on this planet. If you are happy, it shows. It's contagious. It affects everyone who comes into your space. A good laugh massages your insides, lifts your spirits and lightens your step as you walk across the terrain of your life. Happiness and laughter can transform even the bleakest of circumstances into something akin to beauty and healing.

How do we get or find this thing called happiness? Well, we can't buy it, steal it, catch it, chase it, depend on someone else for it, trade it or accidentally lose it. We have to create it—much like an artist creates a beautiful picture on a blank canvas.

Happiness is an art. One of the definitions of art is "creative work." Happiness is nothing else than creative work. How can we go about doing this creative work? First and foremost, it is a matter of attitude—one of hope, of joy, of gratitude even against the greatest of odds. It is a matter of regarding these "odds" as challenges to overcome rather than as self-defeating limits. Second, it is a matter of expansion—of expanding our horizons, seeing new possibilities, trying new ways of doing things and giving the self permission to succeed or to fail. Then like the artist, pick up the brush and do some creative work.

Remember, it is the "pursuit of happiness" we are about. We have to work at it in order to have it and to keep it. It isn't handed to us on a silver platter. Only we, ourselves, can make it happen. Only we know what works for us and brings us the happiness we yearn for, and only we are responsible for choosing it.

*Tiny differences in input today could quickly become inspiring differences in output tomorrow*

—James Gleick

# 17

# You Can Make a Difference

Each of us has the power to make our little corner of the world a better place—thereby affecting the whole world. Yes, each of us has the power to change the world. Each of us is a one-of-a-kind, unique, irreplaceable individual with unique and irreplaceable gifts to offer.

We could all respond to the above with, "Who, me? Change the World? I'm only one person—what can I do?"

Every act of ours has a ripple-effect which moves out in waves touching and affecting people's lives in ways we may never dream of. It may be just a word of encouragement to someone in deep distress which enables another to move on. It may be in becoming a role model—others may say, "If he or she can do it—so can I."

Think of all the "one-persons" who have made a difference during the history of life on this planet: people like Christopher Columbus, George Washington, Abraham Lincoln, Pope John XXIII, Beethoven, Joan of Arc, Michelangelo, Martin Luther King, Mother Teresa, any of your own personal heroes or heroines—or even Adolf Hitler, Josef Stalin or Saddam Hussein. Each of the above is only "one person" like you or me yet each has had a tremendous impact either for good or evil in our world.

Our origins don't matter. Abraham Lincoln was born into poverty grew up in a log cabin yet became president of the US. Mother Teresa was born into a wealthy, privileged family, yet chose to give it all up to become a nun to serve the world's poor and underprivileged. Both went far afield of what might have been expected of them.

I've worked with many, many families with histories of abuse, physical, emotional, verbal, sexual—generations of abuse within their family systems. "The sins of the fathers visited upon the children." Yet, along the family line will come one person who shouts, "Enough! The buck stops here with me!" That "one person" not only changes his or her own personal life, but the lives of that immediate family, all the lives that may come into contact with it and all the future generations following. Think of that ripple effect!

And YOU are "one person." Never consider yourself "less-than" those whose names you see in the headlines, or those who have succeeded in ways you believe you never can. "Bloom where you are planted." Do what you can—right where you are—right this minute.

But how? Or what? you might well ask. We may never know what effect something we do or say may have on another—sometimes for the rest of their lives. For instance, a few years ago I had lunch with a co-worker and a month or so later she called me saying, "I just wanted to call and tell you that the lunch we had together has changed my whole life. It has changed the way I look at things, it has changed my relationships, I can never thank you enough for the ideas and thoughts you shared with me." I was stunned! For the life of me, I could not remember what I could possibly have said that could have made such an impact. I remembered that we had a pleasant time, that I really enjoyed the luncheon but I had no idea whatever of its influence on the quality of her life from then on. We may never know when our actions or examples become a pebble thrown into a pond causing rings of ripples going off into infinity. Following is a poetic illustration of the above: (author unknown)

*It only takes one smile to offer welcome...*

*and blessed be the person who will share it.*

*It only takes one moment to be helpful...*

*and blessed be the person who will spare it.*

*It only takes one joy to lift a spirit...*

*and blessed be the person who will give it.*

*It only takes one life to make a difference...*

*and blessed be the person who will live it.*

Think of a person or persons who by their very presence, friendship and influence have made a big difference in your life. I know there are several in mine, and it's hard to imagine my life without them. Become a positive, one-person, ripple effect—you can make a difference!

*"No man is an island" —John Dunn*

# 18

# A Happy Blessed Easter to All

Springtime is such a beautiful, inspiring time of the year with its seasonal message of birth, new life and of resurrection. There is such a feeling of hope in the air during Springtime. Mother Nature illustrates for us once again in very visible ways—the victory of new life over the death of Wintertime.

As I look out of my window, I see trees budding and blooming, daffodils lifting their lovely yellow heads, tulips, hyacinth brightening the garden and new shoots of green sprouting up all over-new life springing forth everywhere.

The Christian celebration of Easter, the resurrection of Christ after His death on Good Friday communicates the same message of new life, of victory over death, triumph over evil, rebirth and spiritual renewal.

Its lessons also speak of Eternity, of the on-going circle of birth, life, death and resurrection.

There is an Indian legend which moves me to tears every time I read it. It seems so fitting at Easter time.

> A 12-year old boy died of snakebite. The snake's poison robbed him of his life. The grieving parents carried his body to the feet of the tribal Holy man and laid it before him. The three sat silently around the body for a long time.
>
> The father rose, stretched his hands over the feet of the child and said: "All of my life I have not worked for my family as I should have."
>
> And the poison left the feet of the child.
>
> The mother rose, stretched her hands over the heart of the child and said:
>
> "All my life I have not loved my family as I should have."
>
> And the poison left the heart of the child.
>
> The Holy man rose, stretched his hands over the head of the child and said: "All my life I have not believed in the words I have spoken."
>
> And the poison left the head of the child.
>
> And the child rose up.
>
> And the parents and the Holy man rose up.
>
> And life was restored to the village that day.

This beautiful legend speaks of work, of love and of faith and of living them out in daily life.

However, we are all victims of "snake bites" at times. Sometimes we do the biting, sometimes we are bitten. We are all in pain—the pain of not having loved enough, or not being loved enough; the pain of illness or death; the pain of the loss of hope.

We tend to want to deny the pain, to choke it off, to avoid dealing with it. If we can turn and face it, to overcome it or even embrace it as our own Good Friday, we may become able to more fully experience the beauty of Easter Sunday.

"Beauty grips the soul," says Solzhenitsyn. It changes our consciousness, lifts us up, fills us up and expands us - much as the beautiful butterfly emerges from the cocoon into new life. Beauty affects us on many levels, physically, mentally, emotionally and spiritually. Such is the beauty of Easter Morning symbolizing joy, peace and triumph over death.

Reflection on the above story may help us get in touch with the "snake bites" in our lives and bring us to a place of healing and the blessing of a newer, fuller and more abundant, spirit-filled life—a blessed happy Easter season for the rest of our days.

*May life be restored to our village this day.*

# 19

# Are you an Eagle or a Prairie Chicken?

According to an old Indian legend or parable, an Indian brave found an eagle's egg on the bare ground. He placed the egg into the nest of a prairie chicken to give it a chance at life.

A little eaglet hatched with the brood of chicks and grew up with them. All his life he thought and behaved like a prairie chicken because that's all he saw around him and so he believed he was one of them.

He never flexed his great wings because he never even knew he had them or that he had the potential to fly higher and farther than any of those around him.

One day he looked up into the sky and saw a magnificent bird high above him in a cloudless sky. The huge bird was soaring—gliding on the wind's current with such grace of movement that it appeared as though he wasn't even using his great golden wings. "Wow! What a beautiful bird. What is it?" he asked his neighbor. "That's an eagle, the chief of all birds," his neighbor replied. "But don't get any bright ideas or even give it a second thought. You could never be like him."

The young eaglet sighed and continued to scratch in the dirt for seeds and insects as he'd been taught all his life. He grew old and died still believing that he was a prairie chicken.

The moral of this story is, "As ye believe—so ye are!" To quote the great psychologist, William James, "Most people live, whether physically, intellectually or morally, in a very restricted circle of their potential being. They make use of a very small portion of their possible consciousness and of their souls' resources."

Every single day provides opportunities for us to challenge ourselves a little more, to go and grow a little further and to explore new possibilities. But more often we want to play it safe, to stay with what's familiar, afraid to flex our wings. So we just stay on the ground scratching in the dirt. Yet, each dawn brings a new day, a new opportunity, a chance to reach out, to be more, to fly higher. Believe in yourself! There's not another like you in the whole Universe. You are different, you are unique, you are a Child of God, whole, complete and perfect.

**Come on. Flex those wings. Lift yourself off the ground and—**

*SOAR LIKE AN EAGLE!*

# 20

# Loneliness or Solitude

We are all such social beings. We consider ourselves "half of a couple," members of tribes, families, nations and the world. We've been told, "No man is an Island," or "It's not good for man to be alone."

These statements are true, of course—we need mates, families and communities to love, to be loved by and to interrelate with.

However, we also need to be able to live in solitude. That is, to be able to live in peace with oneself, alone, in our own skins. True health and happiness ultimately depends on being able to be alone without feeling lonely. Too often we equate solitude with loneliness and so fill up our alone-time with noise, busyness—anything so we won't be alone with our own thoughts—attempts at avoiding feelings of loneliness.

These feelings don't occur just in isolation or when we are by ourselves. They can happen within marriage, in families, at parties, at work and even in church. Loneliness happens when we have unrealistic expectations that others can take our loneliness away, so we put up with destructive relationships and, tiring or boring friendships. We'd rather suffer those than risk being alone.

No husband, wife, lover, friend or community can ever alleviate our own deep sense of loneliness—because under our skins we are always essentially alone. Not having come to terms with that is often at the root of alcoholism, drug abuse, suicide, crime and psychosomatic illnesses.

Loneliness is a yearning—a "hunger of the heart" for something we can't even define. Some describe it as a kind of homesickness. Shakespeare described it as "immortal longings." However we describe it, it is a universal, human experience and sometimes an excruciating one. It is a longing for life, for belonging, for a spiritual "oneness" we can't quite define.

If no one can take our loneliness away and we can't shift that burden on to someone else—what can we do? Henri J. Nouwen in his book, *Reaching Out* (Doubleday & Co.) says we must convert our loneliness into solitude. The word, "solitude" may imply being alone or isolated, however, it really suggests an inner quality or attitude of the heart. A quiet inner peace that can be maintained no matter how hectic the outer circumstances. Nouwen says, "We must find the courage to enter into the desert of our loneliness and change it by gentle persistent efforts into a garden of solitude." We must face our loneliness, not run from it, deny it, or drown it out. We must learn to become quiet and silent; learn to listen to the whispering of the heart.

Even those in the happiest of relationships, or the most extroverted individuals who seem to thrive and do their best work amidst the company of others need to carve out some alone-time in order to achieve complete fulfillment. It is only in quiet solitude that we can hear the "whispering of the heart." It is during this quiet listening that we can get in touch with the Self within, tune in to the imagination, creativity and the wordless kind of "knowing" that exists within the human heart.

Though we all need our social and intimate relationships in order to have a full life, we also need to find fulfillment that is relevant only to one's self. "To thine own self be true," says Shakespeare's Hamlet. And how else can we find the self to be true to, except in times of quiet solitude. It is at these times when we can become more intimately acquainted with and connected to that person within who is a complete stranger to many.

It is in becoming intimate with that stranger within that we can become really aware of our own needs and how to meet those needs, be they physical, mental, emotional or spiritual. It is in meeting those needs in a mature, caring, responsible way that we can become whole or holy.

From that state of wholeness we can then reach out to our fellow human beings and give of ourselves.

It is when we are alone that we can learn to be who and what we truly are. When we can become comfortable and secure in our own company, we become secure in the world at large. "I never found the companion that was so companionable as solitude" (Henry David Thoreau). "Your heart knows in silence the secrets of the days and nights—your ears thirst for the sounds of your heart's knowledge. The soul unfolds itself like a lotus of countless petals" (Excerpts from *The Prophet*— Kahill Gibran). Our "hearts' knowledge," and the "unfoldment of the soul" is attainable only through solitude.

# 21

# The Trauma of Divorce

Divorce is at the root of many of society's ills. Poverty, domestic violence, crime, poor education, and spiritual malaise often have their origin in the breakdown of the family unit. I don't know of any single life-experience which causes more stress, strain suffering and pain.

Divorce affects every area of personal life—emotionally, physically, psychologically, and spiritually. It affects every area of family life from the infant to the grandparent as well as the extended family of uncles, aunts, and cousins. It affects every area of social life. Communication breaks down and productivity is reduced from the child in the classroom to the parent on the job. It affects every area of spiritual life. Divorced families sometimes experience rejections at Church, their faith in God is diminished; they may no longer find solace in prayer.

A study conducted at the University of Washington prioritized the major stresses in life: death, divorce, loss of job, moving, etc. and their impact on health and well-being. They listed death of a spouse first with divorce as a close second. As a Marriage and Family Therapist, I tend to reverse that order. As a client who had experienced both put it so dryly, "I've gone through both the death of a mate and a divorce and the difference is that in divorce the corpse is still walking around!"

People are often amazed at the depth of their emotional upheaval.

Many express feelings such as, "I'm a basket case! I keep having these awful 'yo-yo' feelings. One minute I'm glad to be out of that mess, and the next I'm crying my eyes out! Will I ever get over this?!" My answer is always, "No, you'll never get over divorce. You may choose to just go through it or you may choose to grow through it, but you'll never get over it. It will always be part of your life experience."

Divorce is a process, not an event. It is not a date on the calendar, which once it has come and gone is over and done with—it does not begin and end with your "day in court." The divorce process has its origin when the relationship first becomes stressful, perhaps years before the actual divorce, and may continue for years afterwards—especially if there are children involved.

It's like walking through a dark forest—you don't know what dangers and perils may lurk there—a very frightening time. But if you walk carefully and take your time, you will come through the dark forest and out into bright sunlight again. Time does heal all wounds.

At times it is not the divorce itself that is so painful, but the "loss of the dream." It's the death or end of hopes and dreams of "living happily ever after" that hurt so much. It's when the "what ifs" and the "if onlys" begin their haunting lament. The sense of loss and disappointment can be overwhelming, bringing poignant feeling of grief, sorrow, rejection, betrayal, failure, despair, depression, anger and loss of self-esteem. All of these emotions must be faced up to and worked through for healing to begin.

Divorce is a very complicated process and it takes its toll. Yet, we have choices—we always have choices. We can grope our way through the darkness and learn nothing or we can grow through it into a new and brighter day. All growth takes time.

It takes time to mourn our losses—it takes time to heal. Form new friendships slowly and take time for little "baby steps" into new ventures.

Don't rush anything. Above all take the time to get reacquainted with yourself—the new you—the new person who is emerging and growing through this most difficult human experience.

# The Stages of Divorce Recovery

Divorce is like going through major surgery. You can't just go about with "business as usual" and expect things to work out; as with surgery, you must take time to recuperate, to rest, to heal, to take good care of yourself or risk prolonged illness or serious illness.

During the initial stages of divorce, people often make one of two choices and these choices will affect their lives for years to come. They can either choose to grow and move on or to remain stuck and become bitter and hardened.

Making the choice to grow through the divorce-experience means to slow down the hectic pace; to take time to become aware of feelings, allowing them to be and to find appropriate ways of expressing them. It means to take an objective look at why the relationship failed without placing any undue blame on self or others—"it takes two to tango." It may mean seeking professional help.

In failing to take the time for all this, people often repeat the same patterns of relationships over and over; making the same mistakes and never understanding, "What keeps going wrong?"

We live in a society where people want an "instant fix." However, all growth takes time and all healing takes time and they do so in developmental stages—divorce recovery is no different! Following are some of the stages people pass through during this process.

## 1) Manage the Damage Stage

The initial stage is a time of acute distress. All you can hope for during this time is to have some kinds of "damage control." Life is in shambles around your ankles. Raging emotions surge through you—sometimes combined with feelings of relief and hope. It can all become very confusing and anxiety-provoking.

Learn to "hang-out" with it. You may even believe you are "going nuts" at times. These are all normal feelings and must be worked through. "This too will pass," and things will begin to even out a bit. Make no major decisions at this time—you may not be able to think straight. Live your daily routine in as normal a way as possible.

## 2) Individuation Stage

Sometime during the first stage you may become aware of a new sense of self-emerging—a person in your own right—not just the other half of a couple. As a woman once told Father Jim Young,

C.S.P. (a pioneer in ministering to the divorced), "When I was a child, I was somebody's daughter, then I became somebody's girlfriend, then I became somebody's wife, then I became somebody's mother. Now that I've become divorced, I've become somebody."

During this stage of recovery you may begin to experience some euphoria, a blind optimism about the future, a premature rushing into a new relationship. Careful! You are not out of the woods yet—you are still in recovery from "major surgery." Doing too much too soon can have disastrous results. Allow this new individual self to grow and blossom, to adjust to a single life-style and become reacquainted with yourself.

## 3) Personal Evolution

As you begin to adjust to your new life, you will also begin to feel more secure within yourself. At this time you may enter a period of growth and development on a deep personal level. This is the time to ask yourself some important, penetrating questions. "What does this failed relationship tell me about myself?" "What do I need in order to be happy?" "What's most important in my life-now—in the immediate future—in the long run?" "Should I move, go back to school, seek a career change?"

It may be time during this third stage to begin new relationships; perhaps to begin dating—but it is not yet time for serious relationships to form. The danger of doing this too soon is that you may find yourself attracted to or by the same kind of relationship that just ended! Decide what qualities and interests you'd like in a future mate; develop those same qualities yourself, and you may bring a person with those qualities and interests into your life. Change always begins with the self.

## 4) A New Sense of Self

As you've moved through the previous stages, learned how to "manage the damage," become more comfortable with the new individual you emerging, become able to assess your own development and personal evolution—you may ask yourself the question "Who am I?" and like the answer. The time of crisis is past and you are now able to make major life decisions with your feet firmly planted on the ground. You know who you are, where you want to go and you are on your way.

How long does this recovery take? It varies from person to person. It takes on an average about four years to recover from the trauma of divorce, to heal and to build life into new patterns. Some need more time, some need less. The greatest danger is in entering into new relationships before the "excess baggage" from the previous one is laid to rest. The divorce rate of these "too-soon" marriages has been estimated at over 80 percent. That's too high a risk to take to go through this agonizing process all over again.

As people take the time to grow through these stages they are often quite surprised at the strength, gifts and talents they never knew they had. Many have said, "Going through this has been hell on earth, and much as I hate to say it, it's the best thing that's ever happened to me."

It's not as much what happens to us that matters as much as what we do with what happens.

# You Don't Divorce the Kids

"What about the kids?" is perhaps the most difficult and perplexing question a divorcing couple faces. Divorce ranks as one of the highest causes of anxiety and pain in life—especially for children. It has been estimated that each year over a million children are affected by divorce in this country. In fact, divorce has become so commonplace that there is a danger that we may become insensitive to the all-pervading "angst" that divorce brings into their young lives.

Yet, there are times when divorce is the only viable answer to stressful and destructive family relationships. Too often, parents have stayed together "for the kids" when it would have been far healthier for all concerned to separate. On the other hand, too many parents throw in the towel before exploring all options to see whether the marriage and family could have become reconciled. As all parents know, parenting is hard work, and it doesn't get any easier trying to go it alone in two separate households.

Adults often assume that children are "mini-adults" who are able to perceive situations that seem so obvious. Not so! Children see things through different colored glasses. Divorce often causes overwhelming feelings of powerlessness in children. They may feel rage, despair, shame, fear, and hopelessness about their future and don't have a clue as to how to cope with these feelings. They may bring a parent's ire down upon their heads with inappropriate behavior or other expressions of their deep emotions.

Some children will act out with aggressive behavior both at home and at school. Others will become silent and withdrawn. Some will regress to earlier behaviors such as bed-wetting, thumb-sucking, whining and so one. Infants and very young children may become listless and sad.

Parents may assume that the child who is silent, withdrawn or non-reacting has adjusted and accepted the situation, which may be totally inaccurate. The child may simply be unable to, or doesn't feel safe enough, to communicate what's going on within. It may be just too scary to the child—especially if the parents themselves seem insecure and afraid. Age and maturity level will greatly determine the child's reactions. Infants and toddlers may become irritable and restless. They may not know cognitively what's going on but they can easily pick up their parents' emotional tones. They may also be grieving the absence of the absent parent.

Children under five often react out of sheer bewilderment, trying to figure out what's going on. Those between six and eight often feel guilty and assume that they did something to cause the divorce. Kids between ten and twelve may experience great anger and may express themselves in either angry outbursts or depression. Teenagers tend to become more outspoken, critical and try to bluff their way in a cocky, know-it-all fashion. On the surface, teens may appear to be somewhat mature and self-sufficient, but like the younger ones, they desperately need the assurance of their parents' love.

Divorce can become a time of healing, growth, and better communications for all concerned. However, in order for that to happen, parents need to clue their kids into what's going on and give them age-appropriate information. Don't overwhelm them with too much information which they don't have the maturity to handle; or not enough information causing needless fear and panic. Never keep them guessing about where and with whom they will live. Fear of abandonment may be very strong within them.

Affirm their feelings using phrases like, "Yes, I know you are scared. I'm scared too. This is a very scary time for all of us. But we'll get through it OK; you'll see." Never downplay their fears and anxieties; that will only make them more afraid and anxious. Above all, they need to know that even though their parents are divorcing each other—they are not divorcing them.

Kids are loyal little creatures, and their sense of loyalty may create confusion and frustration for them. They feel connected to both parents and may fear that if they express loyalty to one, they are being disloyal to the other. Never, ever "bad-mouth" a parent in a child's presence—no matter what the circumstances might be. Doing so only causes more anxiety, and the kids may apply the negative comments to themselves.

Remarks such as "You're just like your father (or mother)" in an angry or hostile tone of voice can diminish the child's own self-esteem and affront his or her sense of loyalty.

Discipline is vitally important and can become quite troublesome during the transitional stages of divorce. The "ground-rules" put into place at this time pave the way for future parent-child interactions. As much as possible, have the same set of rules in both parents' households. Never allow one parent to become "Santa" and the other the "heavy." Kids are smart, and soon even the little ones can figure out how to work one parent against the other in order to get their own way.

In summary, to lessen the negative impact of divorce on your children, respect and affirm their feelings; listen to their worries and concerns and try to ease them. Assure them of your constant love and support and don't neglect the discipline.

Parenting doesn't end with divorce—it just takes a little more planning.

# 22

# Remarriage—Making it Work

Divorce statistics are alarmingly high in general and even more so for second marriages.

There are two major reasons for the high (80 percent) percentage of failures in second (and subsequent) marriages: first, marrying too soon after divorce or widowhood, and second, marrying before one is fully aware of potential problems. Old habits and attitudes, which may be unhealthy for the new relationship, may be carried over from the previous one if they haven't been worked through.

After divorce or widowhood, people are often intensely lonely, especially if they have never lived alone. This loneliness can be very threatening and at first almost unbearable. There is an intense need to re-couple, to be part of something or someone outside of oneself. These two factors alone can drive the newly single person into a hasty, unsatisfactory and unsuccessful marital relationship.

Many enter into a second marriage before they are emotionally and psychologically healed from the scars of a failed relationship—before they are ready to make the commitments necessary to make any relationship work. Widowed persons with memories of a happy marriage may have unrealistic expectation of a second marriage—expecting it to take up where the other left off. Divorce and widowhood are major life crises, necessitating major life changes. Like any crisis they require enough time to elapse for a full recovery before moving on to the next phase of life.

# Recovery is hard work

A) It requires honest self-evaluation and coping with one's feelings which often run rampant.

B) It requires forgiveness and letting go of the past.

C) It requires taking responsibility for one's own happiness without placing that as a burden on the shoulders of another.

D) Recovery may require professional help in helping gain distance and objectivity. Sometimes the "pebbles in one's path" become huge stumbling stones if we don't tread the path with care.

Unfortunately, many people regard their new single state as only a transition time—a waiting period between marriages—rather than a time for personal growth and personal evolvement. William Bridges, in his book, *Transitions* (Addison-Wesley Publishing Co.) speaks about the "Neutral Zone" between endings and new beginnings. This important neutral zone is often short-changed. If we will take the time to allow ourselves to be in this neutral zone long enough, we can learn how to be alone without becoming lonely; to take the opportunity to discover what we really want out of life. In order to do that we must take the time between the ending of the old and the beginning of the new to sort things out, to "see from a distance" what worked and what didn't so that past mistakes are not repeated.

Besides marrying too soon, second marriages often fail because people don't take into consideration the complex issues that may come along with the marriage vows the second time around. These include previous marital history, children and step-children, custody agreements, child-support payments, present and former in-laws, religious beliefs, established life-style habits—just to mention a few! None of which were part of the package of the first marriage but which must be addressed in order to make a second union work.

On the positive side, we can and do learn from past experiences and mistakes to work more effectively in relationships. Hopefully we learn to be more discerning and make better choices in picking a life-partner. After the initial period of adjustment in family life, children in remarried families generally do as well as those in first families—providing their needs are met and they aren't forced into divided loyalties.

Perhaps the best indicator of a happy second marriage is freedom of choice. Do you feel free to not remarry and still be happy? If so, you've attained a sense of confidence, a good self-esteem and the capacity to find happiness on your own. If you feel a desperate need or pull to remarry, it's best to spend some more time in the "neutral zone." It is only when we can freely choose (not need) to share our lives intimately with another that we have a real chance at happiness.

Let love be "a moving sea between the shores of your souls"—allowing each person the freedom to become their own person—"to sing and dance together and be joyous—yet let each of you be alone." "For the oak tree and the cypress grow not in each other's shadow" (*The Prophet*, Kahill Gibran).

To make any marriage work and especially a second marriage requires maturity and a willingness to learn from the past—allowing the partner to be who he or she is and permitting the same for the self. It requires the desire and the capacity to grow as individuals and as a unit; to be able to let go of the past and share a vision for the future while at the same time being totally at home in the present. It takes commitment "in sickness and in health, "physically, mentally, and spiritually. It requires faith, trust, patience, and forbearance. Above all it requires love and forgiveness and the ability to express them.

It has been said that "Marriage may be the closest to heaven we can get in this life—but it can also be the closest to hell!" A good marriage doesn't just "happen." It is created and maintained by ever-vigilant attention, mutual sharing and abiding love—in God, self and others.

## 23

# The Blended Family: Becoming Stepparents

I often wonder about the origin of words, such as stepmother, stepfather, stepchild. Could the meaning have been "a step away from the 'real' thing?" Those can be rather frightening words—evoking scenes from the old fairy tales about "wicked stepmothers."

Someone coined the term "The Blended Family" rather Х than using the term, "Step Family." It's a lot friendlier and much more descriptive—a "blending" of parts of former family units into a new family unit. A "family" is much more than a just group of people living together. Being a family involves commitment to all its members, total involvement and interest in each other's lives past, present and future and at the same time fostering individuality and independence. Yet forming this new family unit is not for the "faint of heart." A new marriage, where one or both partners has children from a previous marriage, is faced at its very beginning with many more potential difficulties and problems in just living out ordinary daily life than the nuclear family which began together.

Couples entering a new marital relationship along with a ready-made family may be so anxious to have everybody get along, they bend over backwards to become a "super-mom" or a "super-dad." They well understand the trauma involved with the kids, the stress and strain of divided loyalties, adjustment to new surroundings and new relatives.

They do all they can to make things work. In doing so, they may forget to be attentive to the most important relationship of all—that between the spouses. With all the emotional complications and needs of the new blended family, they may not spend enough time and energy to build a strong marital relationship. This is the primary bond. If the relationship between the parents is strong and healthy, their love and affection for each other will build a safe and secure nest for the kids to thrive in.

The first problem may be one of bonding, or relating. Children feel bonded to their natural parents and may deeply resent having a "new" parent thrust upon them. Even though the family of origin may have been very unhappy and dysfunctional, they still want their own parents together and may act out in ways to try to sabotage the new relationships. Much depends on how the idea (of the new marriage) is presented to them. If time is allowed for everyone to become well acquainted, if they are included in the plans, and develop a feeling of belonging, of being an important part of the new family unit, they will look forward to a new life, adjust and be happy. If on the other hand, they are just introduced to someone with, "This is going to be your new mom or dad" out of the blue, there will be trouble from Day One!

Love cannot be "taught;" it must be "caught." Children can't learn to love without first experiencing it. They have to be shown, to have it modeled for them. In the tentative first days of the new family unit, it is natural to be nervous and apprehensive; allowances need to be made for that. Parents must be patient, comforting, reassuring, understanding, flexible, yet firm, and disciplined. It is a monumental task.

Love, determination, and a good sense of humor will carry you a long way, but it is essential that parents have realistic expectations. There won't be perfect harmony all the time; bonding and affection don't spring up overnight. Disruptions and rebellions will occur. It takes time to blend—to become "family." And even when it does appear to be blending well—there will be "those" times. There will be times of rivalry between siblings. There will be times when they'll shout, "It's unfair!" and believe they are on the short end of the stick. There will be jealousies, especially if a new baby enters the picture.

Then there are the times when children visit the non-custodial parent and come home stressed out, angry, belligerent, or teary. Often the child's chaotic emotions are due to a divided sense of loyalty, feeling guilty about "abandoning" the other parent. Maybe there are different rules with the other parent. All this can be terribly confusing especially for a younger child. Give them time and space to readjust. Explain the reasons for the feelings and encourage them to talk about them.

Above all, be real—don't "buy" the kids with gifts, bribes, or promises you may not be able to keep. Don't condone behavior you wouldn't permit under normal circumstances. Have family meetings where family rules are discussed, make sure everyone understands what the rules are; and knows in advance what the rewards or consequences are for compliance or non-compliance.

Given all of the above, stepparenting may appear to be a formidable task, indeed. However, given enough time with patience and understanding, mutual bonds of affection, trust and intimacy will develop, and relating to each other harmoniously will become the norm. Allow the time needed to really get acquainted on a deeper level, to get to know each other's quirks, likes and dislikes.

How long will all this take? It varies from family to family, but it takes at least a year before all members begin to function as a unit; maybe even two to three years before it feels like "family." Take the time for everyone "settle in" and find a comfortable pattern and style of being together.

And, parents, above all, need to remember to be attentive to their own spousal relationship, for without a firm marital foundation, it won't work.

# 24

# The Hand that Rocks the Cradle Rules the World

Parenting is not an easy task—an understatement if there ever was one! Just ask me, I know!

As a mother of six, grandmother of fourteen and great-grandmother of four—along with my many years as a Marriage and Family Therapist—I know whereof I speak!

There are four basic principles of parenting I subscribe to. While they may not always be easy to live out, they may serve as guidelines or a roadmap on this vitally important highway to the future.

## Four Principles of Parenting

### 1. Unconditional Love

In order to grow into adults with a good self-esteem and sense of worth, children must know without a doubt that they are loved! They are loved—no matter what! They are loved, if they are "good, bad, or somewhere in between"—again no matter what! They aren't loved ONLY if they behave themselves and obey all the rules—they are loved just because they ARE! In a loving environment, children feel free to make mistakes, to succeed sometimes, to fail sometimes, and to learn from both experiences. And, children learn to love, only if they experience love.

## 2. A Good Moral Value System

Children will adopt the value system of the adults around them, parents, teachers, and leaders in the community. Good, sound morals are "caught not taught." You cannot teach a child to be honest and truthful if you, yourself, are not so. If you don't obey the laws, if you brag about getting away with something—don't expect your child to be any different. Model yourself after the kind of person you want your child to become. You cannot teach your child to love God and neighbor if you never demonstrate those values by act, word, and deed in your own life.

## 3. Boundary Setting

Boundary setting is only another term for good old-fashioned discipline. The word, "discipline" comes from the word, "disciple," and the dictionary defines a "disciple" as a pupil, learner, follower. "To discipline" is defined as "to instruct, to train, or to educate" one to become a disciple. What do we want our children, the citizens of tomorrow, to be disciples of? We must decide—as parents and educators—for the responsibility is ours! If children are taught not only to obey the rules; but understand the REASONS for the rules; know in advance the rewards for compliance, and the consequences for non-compliance, they learn to set their own limits or boundaries. From this grows self-discipline and maturity. Mere blind obedience does not foster creativity, responsibility, or good citizenship, it only creates robots!

## 4. Consistency

Inconsistency on the part of parents creates more confusion in the minds of children than anything else I can imagine. Your kids need to know where you stand, and where you stand should be a "constant"—not something that changes with your mood. I remember when my two older sons were about 10 and 11, the younger one was nagging me about letting him do something and he was very persistent—determined to wear me down. Finally his older brother called him aside and said quietly, "You are wasting your breath, I've tried everything you have, it won't work, so knock it off." He did. If I'd given in, it would have been all over! Next time the refrain would have been, "But you let me last time, how come not this time?", or the older one would have said, "How come you let him and not me!" But sometimes it is SO tempting just to give in—you are tired, worn out, and think, "Oh well JUST this one time it won't hurt"—Oh yes it DOES—because then it will never again be "just this one time." History will keep repeating itself.

Have as few "No's" as possible. I once saw a poster asking, "Is your child being raised in a NO-Storm?" with a small child surrounded with the words "no-no, no-no." Think over your "No's" very carefully, explain them as clearly as possible, and then stand firm. Be very clear about the consequences if rules are broken, and act swiftly (not necessarily angrily) if they are. Never allow your own mood of the moment to throw you off the track so that you become too rigid or too wishy-washy. Focus on the positive aspects of disciplines; rewards, praise and affirmation work wonders.

As a parent, you are the architect of the future. The years fly by so quickly—too quickly—and the future is here before you know it! Refine your blueprints to tomorrow—while there is still time!

# 25

# Love That Teenager!

Teenagers are such wonderful and unpredictable people. Sometimes they are sweet and lovable; other times they are downright unreasonable, frustrating, demanding, and irrational.

You may wonder who's losing their mind—you or them! You may also wonder if they have regressed back to the "terrible twos." In a way, they have. The two-year-old toddler is teetering back and forth between infancy and childhood. One moment he is the sweet charming baby and the next a little tyrant screaming, "NO!" to your every request.

The teenager teeters between childhood and young adulthood, having just emerged from the more placid latency stage of development into the tyrant again screaming, "No!" Frustrating as this may be, this too will pass.

Life is a series of cycles, infancy, childhood, teenage adolescence, young adulthood, mature adulthood, middle age, and old age. All stages have their developmental norms, and it is very helpful to understand these stages as you and your loved ones grow through these stages.

The teenager, like the toddler, is making a push toward independence, attempting to define himself or herself as separate from the parent and the rest of society. Trying to figure out who you are, where you are going, what life's all about is difficult at any age, but perhaps the most difficult during the time of adolescence.

Major changes take place during this time: physical and hormonal changes in the body along with strong emotional responses to everything. Worry about school, uncertainty about the future, coping with peer pressure, relating with their families, changing value systems—all of these and more plague the teenager. No wonder there's rebellion. It's like traveling through a foreign land, not knowing the language or customs and trying to make sense of it all.

The teen years are a time of transition, and transitions are always fraught with turmoil and change. Teenagers are children in transition not yet young adults even though they may view themselves as quite grown-up and wanting grown-up privileges—and they want them without the responsibilities that go with privileges. They are not mature enough to know, or care, that privileges and responsibility go hand in hand—especially in the earlier teen years of about age 13 to 16.

That's where the parent comes in. Parents often make the mistake of viewing the teenager as a "junior adult." Your teenager may be bigger than you, stronger than you, maybe even smarter than you, but emotionally that person is still a child—much of the time needing guidance, love and assurance from you as the parent.

A parent's first responsibility is to provide a loving, happy home life. The bond between the parents themselves is the strongest base for security in children and teenagers. Whether in a single-parent family or a two-parent family, the teenager needs to experience unconditional love. That means the parent will always be there no matter what, There can be no, "I'll love you if..." or "I'll love you when..."

One of the easiest and most neglected ways to express feelings is through eye contact. A look of affection and caring  expresses much more than words ever can. A gentle touch is also a wonderful communicator.

In addition to unconditional love, teenagers also need authority figures and good role models. The boundaries and limits set by authority give teens a sense of security—as much as they may rebel against it. It also prepares them for the boundaries that society will place upon them. Rebellion is a normal kind of limit-testing, a necessary trying out of the wings to see how far they can fly. Yet they also need to know  that, if they fly out too far, someone will care enough to call a halt and reel them back in.

My kids used to call me the "meanest mom on the block" when I wouldn't permit them to do what "all the other kids are doing." However, I also noted a sense of pride and security, even while they were complaining, "*Our* folks won't let us do that."

Eye contact is vital. Just one look can stop someone in his tracks. My husband coined a phrase that had a powerful impact: "It's time for an eyeball gathering." That meant sitting down at the table, "eyeball to eyeball" for some serious discussion.

They hated it. When we'd say, "It's time for an eyeball gathering—the time and place is up to you," the kids would invariably want to do it NOW and get it over with!

Family rules need to be consistent and not just exercised at the parent's whim or mood. The breaking of a rule must have consequences that are spelled out explicitly in  advance and swiftly enforced. A rule without predictable consequences is a rule without impact—and one that will not be taken seriously.

Today's teenager faces more challenges and choices than any other youngsters ever have in history. As they face these challenges and choices they need a parent to be there when needed, to be calm when their emotions run rampant; to be stable when they feel insecure, to be firm and set appropriate boundaries when they want to run amuck, to be a teacher of sound moral and spiritual values; to be an exemplary role model and to set a good example. Rather a tall order!

The importance of being a good role model cannot be overstated.

Be what you wish your sons or daughters to be. If you expect them to be courteous, be so yourself. If you want your child not to abuse alcohol or drugs, don't allow them to see you out of control with substance abuse. If you wish them to have a relationship with God, share yours with them. If you want them to have religious affiliation, go with them to the church of your choice—don't just send them. Children learn and emulate what they see and experience.

And remember—

*The apple doesn't fall far from the tree!*

## 26

# Help Your Child Learn to Make Responsible Decisions

Becoming a responsible adult means to become a responsible decision-maker, and the time to begin learning how to do that is in childhood, early childhood—maybe even babyhood.

A ten-month-old infant can be taught to make decisions and live with the consequences. Offer the child two or three toys. When the baby chooses one, remove the others. Of course, you don't want to overwhelm a very young child with too many choices or a decision that may be too difficult. Keep choices simple and age-appropriate.

Affirm your child's decisions with words like, "Good choice!" If your response is, "Now are you sure about that? Wouldn't you rather do this?" the child will vacillate back forth, and may finally burst into tears, crying, "I can't make up my mind—you choose." If youngsters are never given the opportunity to make their own choices and decisions—even about which cereal to have for breakfast, or what colors to choose, they will never become able to make firm decisions about anything. One day your child will become the adult who says, "I have such a hard time making decisions!" or, "I just can't make up my mind about anything!"

This person goes through life unable to take responsibility for life, always depending on others for validation of their choices.

Along with decision making comes living with the consequences, another valuable lesson to learn early in life. My grandmother used to say, "You made your bed, now lie in it!"— meaning, you made your choices, now deal with them! If your child knows a rule, knows what the consequences are, yet deliberately breaks the rule, the child has made a decision and must live with the consequences. It was the youngster's choice, not yours, a fact you may need to point out. If the consequences of the choice are not labeled as "punishment" but rather as a logical outcome of a given behavior, your child will learn to take responsibility for what happens as a result of that behavior.

When children are affirmed and encouraged to make their own independent decisions at an early age, they are far more capable to cope with the bigger choices and decisions they face as they become teenagers and young adults. They will feel much more secure in their own abilities and have a good sense of self worth. They will also become less likely to give in to peer pressure.

It is sad but true that even before their teen years, many children may face choices about the use of drugs or alcohol. They may be pressured by their peers to become sexually active at an early age, or to drop out of school. With a strong value system and decision-making skills, our kids will be better prepared to make healthy choices about everything in their lives, from study habits, to how to spend their spare time, or who their friends will be.

If we want strong responsible leaders tomorrow, their training begins in the cradle today!

*Train children in the right way, and when old
they will not stray.—Proverbs 22:6.*

# 27

# The Children of the World—Who Protects Them?

As we are about to begin a new century, let us think of those who are just beginning their lives, the children of the world, this planet's most valuable resource, the hope of a better tomorrow.

I'm thinking of my great-grandchildren and wondering what their lives will be like, surely a lot different from yours or mine! I'm also thinking of all those other little ones of the world—those who know only hunger, poverty, abuse.

Following is a copy of a document which we should all read and ponder upon as we enter a New Year, and vow to do whatever we can to see that its mandates are carried out.

## The UN Declaration of Rights of the Child

—The right to affection, love and understanding.

—The right to adequate nutrition and medical care.

—The right to free education.

—The right to full opportunity for play and recreation.

—The right to a name and nationality.

—The right to special care, if handicapped.

—The right to be among the first to receive relief in times of disaster.

—The right to be a useful member of society and to develop individual abilities.

—The right to be brought up in a spirit of peace and universal brotherhood.

—The right to enjoy these rights, regardless of race, creed, sex, national or social origin.

Note that this document speaks of these as "rights" for all the children of the world, not just the "privileges" of a few. Such a declaration coming from the United Nations is indeed impressive. If only it were universally heeded. Yet even the fact that such a document exists gives us hope. It shows that there is global awareness of how things ought to be, and awareness is the prerequisite for change.

The statistics of the abuse of children—be it verbal, physical, psychological or sexual—is staggering! No one can estimate the percentage of teenage or adult violent behavior, (or even wars) which can be laid at the feet of child abuse. Some experts flatly state that the correlation stands at 100 percent—that, if the perpetrators of violence were not themselves victims of abuse as children, at least they lived in an environment in which violence was the "norm" and as a result became desensitized.

We must take these "UN Declarations" to heart. We must honor those rights in our homes, our schools, our neighborhoods and across the planet. We must take it upon ourselves to protect our children. We must do what we can to bind the wounds of those already wounded. If we don't, history will keep repeating itself generation after generation as it has for centuries. We must, or there may come a time when we won't be able to celebrate the dawning of a new year, much less a new century.

# 28

# Children Learn from Experience

In order to insure that we have capable, responsible, emotionally secure, and stable leaders in tomorrow's world, we need to provide today's children with positive, affirming experiences.

"Experience is the best teacher" for all of us, and especially for children. Children learn how to be in their world from what they experience in their world.

Consider the following: (quoted from Christopher Notes)

**If a child—**

> **Lives with criticism he learns to condemn.**
>
> **Lives with hostility, she learns to fight.**
>
> **Lives with ridicule, he learns to be shy.**
>
> **Lives with shame, she learns to feel guilty.**
>
> **Lives with tolerance, he learns to be patient.**

**Lives with encouragement, she learns confidence.**

**Lives with praise, he learns to appreciate.**

**Lives with fairness, she learns justice.**

**Lives with security, he learns to have faith.**

**Lives with approval, she learns to like herself.**

**Lives with acceptance and friendship, he learns to find love in the world.**

Since the primary way that children learn life's lessons is by what they see and experience, it is imperative that parents, teachers, clerics, community leaders model responsible behavior, show love and concern for them, for themselves, for the community and the world at large.

You are the role model, the example setter, the shaper of tomorrow's world. Oh, sure, the kids may spend their time idolizing the latest music group, the movie star, the athlete, their peer group, and not give you—the parent or teacher—the time of day. But rest assured, the primal influence is much closer to home—YOU! That is truly an awesome challenge and responsibility!

All of the world's greatest leaders, artists, scientists were at one time someone's little child. Abraham Lincoln's famous quote, "All that I am and hope to be, I owe to my angel mother" is a wonderful tribute to the positive role of parenting.

Listen sometime to the lyrics of the song, "The Cat's in the Cradle"—I mean really listen. "I'm gonna be like you Dad, I'm gonna be just like you." It's downright scary!

Be what you want your children to emulate. Don't just tell them the kind of persons you hope and dream they will be.

Be the role model—show them.

"There's always one moment in childhood when the door opens and lets the future in." (Graham Greene). We, the adults in a child's life, are the custodians of that door.

# 29

# Happy Birthday USA, July 4th

"We hold these truths to be self-evident, that all men are created equal, that they are endowed by their Creator with certain unalienable rights, that among these are Life, Liberty and the pursuit of Happiness."—Thomas Jefferson.

As we once again celebrate our country's birthday on July 4th, it behooves us to remember the above quotation taken from the Declaration of Independence in Congress on July 4, 1776. It was a unanimous declaration of that Congress, representing the will of the original thirteen states of the United States of America.

Far too often we forget the tremendous impact those few words have had, not only in our country, but on the whole world community. And, perhaps, we also take those "unalienable rights" too much for granted—almost as much as we do the air we breathe. Freedom of speech, freedom of the press, freedom of religion, freedom of thought and education—all these in addition to "life, liberty and the pursuit of happiness" are part and parcel of what we believe is the "good life" in America.

It was not always so in the past, and it is not always so in the present. It is the ideal, but not always lived out in reality. Freedom and rights are often denied to different segments and populations of our society. If we wish the ideal to be more "present" in our present, and preserved for future generations we must be ever vigilant and guard against the erosion of all peoples' "inalienable rights."

The wisdom and knowledge of the pioneering forefathers of our country constantly amazes me. If you read the Declaration of Independence and the Constitution in the context of the life and times they were written, it is truly astounding!

It would do us all some good to review that part of this country's history from time to time in order to really appreciate the freedom and liberty we enjoy today. It's hard to imagine the lives of the colonists, the hardships they endured, and the social and religious persecutions they experienced. They worked long and hard to come up with a new kind of Government—"of the people—by the people—for the people."

Every year as we set off the fireworks in celebration of the birth of this great country of ours, let us remember Jefferson's words, and let us resolve to protect the rights and freedoms of all our peoples, of every race, nationality and creed. As we sing, "My Country 'tis of thee, sweet land of liberty," let us really mean it. Let us do all that we can to make it a "sweet land of liberty" for all within its borders.

Every Fourth of July, it would behoove us all to remember Lincoln's words in the opening and closing of his Gettysburg Address.

> *Four score and seven years ago*
> *our fathers brought forth on this continent,*
> *a new nation, conceived in liberty*
> *and dedicated to the proposition that*
> *all men are created equal...*
>
> *—that this nation, under God*
> *shall have a new birth of freedom.*
> *And that the government of the people,*
> *for the people and by the people,*
> *shall not perish from the earth.*

**GOD BLESS AMERICA!**

# 30

# Silly Geese? We Should Be So Silly!

On any given day here at the beach, we can see and hear a flock of geese flying in formation overhead. They are so orderly and organized in their flight patterns—it's amazing. As we watch and marvel, we wonder why they fly that way.

Research into the habits of our fine-feathered friends has shown us that as each bird flaps its wings, it creates an updraft of air for the bird immediately following. This permits the following bird to fly with much less effort and fatigue. By flying in a "V" formation, a whole flock can add at least 71 percent greater flying range than if each bird flew alone.

Whenever a goose falls out of formation, it feels the drag and resistance of trying to go it alone and quickly gets back into formation in order to take advantage of the lifting power of the bird immediately in front of it. When the lead-goose gets tired, it rotates back, and another goose takes up the lead and flies point. The geese honk from the rear to encourage the others up front to keep up the good work. I've heard that they even allow tiny hummingbirds to "hitch a ride" when they migrate.

If one of the flock becomes ill or is wounded by gunshot and falls out of formation, two geese fall with him and follow him to the ground to help or protect him. He is not abandoned, they will stay with him until he is either able to fly again or dies. Then they will set out on their own or with another flock's formation to catch up with their own group.

Every spring at the beach on the North Bay, I've observed an enormous, beautiful gander strutting back and forth. He doesn't fly away as I approach. Rather, he stands his ground, observes me, then slowly walks away, looking back occasionally—watching. And I know—somewhere close by—in the opposite direction to the one he is walking—his mate is sitting on her nest starting their little family. He is standing guard, being the protector.

Now where did the term "silly goose" come from? Nothing of the above seems in the least bit silly! Think of all the problems, loss of time and energy we could save if we didn't try to "fly alone" but lived and worked in such an organized, cooperative way. Our productivity would skyrocket, and there would be fewer lonely people in the world. Their "honking" is done in encouragement—not, "Hey you, get out of my way!" They take turns at leadership, so that no one has to bear the burden all the time.

They take care of their ill and wounded and display a compassionate care we could do well to emulate. The father stands guard and protects his family—there is no separation or divorce; geese mate for life.

In our "wise and all-knowing human wisdom," we could learn much about how to live by observing and adopting some of Mother Nature's Wisdom. If we could become as "silly" as the goose, we might live in a much happier world.

# 31

# The Listening Art

Daily, we are called upon to listen...to listen to a spouse, a child, a parent, siblings, co-workers, friends, neighbors—all those with whom we come into contact.

Good listening skills have the potential of enriching all aspects of one's life—our intimate relationships, as well as social or work-related relationships, and our prayer life.

There are many ways to listen—to really listen. Effective listening involves more than just hearing with our ears. It requires alert attention using the whole body, the eyes, voice, body movement, and posture. How disconcerting it is to be talking to someone and see the other person's eyes roaming all over the room and never connecting with you. You feel about as important as a bothersome gnat! A body turned away is a mind turned away. Face the person you are listening to with your shoulders turned toward him or her. If seated, turn your knees toward the person. All these seemingly small things contribute a great deal to the feeling of being valued and heard.

Prayer without listening is a one-way conversation. It's like calling God on the phone, speaking your "piece" and then hanging up. God's reply is quiet and subtle; without keen listening you will never hear the answer.

## Hints for developing the art of listening:

—**Take the time needed; it is time well spent.**

—**Show interest, make eye contact, connect with the person.**

—**Give your full attention, with ears, eyes, voice tone, and body language.**

—**Listen for feelings, hear "between the lines" to what is not being spoken.**

—**Ask questions for clarification; don't assume you know.**

—**Allow the speaker to finish a thought without interruption.**

—**Give feedback when the speaker has indicated he/ she is ready for it.**

—**Keep confidential matters private.**

—**Be respectful; honor the person's thoughts and feelings.**

—**Practice often**

—**Keep on working on ways to improve your listening skills.**

Empathic listening is not a passive act. It is active, dynamic, and involved. I can think of nothing more affirming than to have someone attentively listening to me. It warms the heart and the soul.

***To truly hear someone is to heal.***

# 32

# Watch Your Tongue!

Never underestimate the power of the spoken word! The Book of Proverbs (18:21) says, "Death and life are in the power of the tongue; and they that love it shall eat the fruit thereof."

Our habits of speech, the words we use daily, the meanings we attach to our words, the tone of voice we use as we express them all have incredible impact on those who hear them. Consider the emotional effect on you when someone speaks to you pleasantly in a soft soothing voice compared to your reaction when one is angrily shouting obscenities. The former helps you become more relaxed; the latter makes you cringe and want to run or to shout back.

The responsible use of the tongue begins with responsible thought, for language begins with thought. As you think, so shall you speak. Sigmund Freud insisted that there was no such thing as a "slip of the tongue," that somehow, in some way, we really mean what we say in a "Freudian slip" even though we may not be consciously aware of it. Before we can watch our tongues, however, we must watch our thoughts—for our tongues will betray us in a weak moment.

Take custody of your thoughts, and you will be able to govern your tongue. If you deliberately choose to harbor only positive, kind, encouraging thoughts you won't be likely to speak in negative, hostile or discouraging manner. Thoughts fuel feelings and feelings fuel thoughts and both are eventually expressed in words, often much to our regret. How often we find ourselves saying, "I wish I hadn't said that!" "I'd give anything to be able to take those words back!" "I didn't mean it!" Once said, they can't be unsaid. They are out there and can't be recalled. They smart, hurt, and linger even with the most profuse apologies.

The opening paragraph states, "death and life are in the power of the tongue." Words like, "I love you—I care about you," are life-giving and nurturing while words like, "I hate you—you make me sick!" are death-dealing and destructive. The words we speak affect our lives and that of others on many levels—the physical, mental, emotional and spiritual.

Our habitual use of thought and tongue determines how we will "eat the fruit thereof"—whether it tastes sweet or bitter is up to us.

*He hath a heart as sound as a bell, and his tongue is the clapper; for what his heart thinks his tongue speaks.*

*"Much Ado About Nothing"—Shakespeare*

## 33

# Depression: Its Symptoms and Management

Depression is a major mental and emotional health problem in America. Most of us suffer from this affliction in varying degrees from time to time— ranging from a mild case of the "blues" to severe psychosis. It is almost a universal condition and is no "respecter of persons."

Depression strikes people in all walks of life, the rich and the poor, the young and the old, the educated and the illiterate, those who appear to "have the world by the tail," and those whose lives seem to be "going to hell in a hand basket."

There are many and varied causes of depression. These may include: Disappointment or unrealistic expectations of self, of others, or of their environment; low self-esteem in comparison with others; grief, death, divorce or loss of any kind; illness or disability; feelings of rejection or perceived lack of appreciation; anxiety or fear; anger overtly unexpressed; lack of achievable goals—nothing to look forward to; aging, physical, chemical or hormonal causes—such as postpartum depression or menopause. These do not necessarily cause depression, for many experience these conditions without becoming unduly depressed, but they are often triggering events or situations.

All of us get "down in the dumps" at times when things don't go as we'd liked or hoped they would. Sometimes we just need an "attitude adjustment" to pull ourselves out of it. Other times we may need some help. Recognizing some of the symptoms of depression will help us identify it and also help us to become able to manage our lives better.

## Symptoms of depression

—**Loss of pleasure or interest in things usually enjoyed**

—**Loss of appetite or over-eating**

—**Insomnia or hypersomnia**

—**Fatigue or loss of energy**

—**Diminished ability to think or concentrate**

—**Feelings of worthlessness or hopelessness**

—**Lack of a sense of purpose in life or goals**

—**Sadness, tears welling up often**

There are a number of things we can do to lift ourselves out of these conditions which can diminish the quality of life. We can take advantage of some of nature's "anti-depressants" such as walking on the beach, in the meadow, woods, or mountains; to enjoy simple things such as the birds' singing, the wind blowing across your face and through your hair; looking at the stars on a clear night, watching the moon rise, etc.

For some other possible "cures" or management of the above symptoms you might try some of the following:

—**Look for things you like about yourself—make a list of your own special unique talents. Enjoy your successes and achievements, set some new realistic achievable goals.**

—**Reach out to others, phone friends with interests in common with yours. Make social engagements you can't easily back out of— invite them to your house for an evening. Do it even if you don't feel inclined to do so.**

—**Seek out people who are interesting and energetic. Make the extra effort—attend sports events, a jazz festival, go dancing, swimming, skiing or hiking. Act as if you really enjoy it and soon you will. In other words, "Fake it 'til you make it!"**

—**Watch a comedy, read a funny book, read just for fun. Avoid heavy dramas or serious books.**

—**Be especially attentive to your meals; make them interesting, unusual, and nutritious. But** don't over-do it—just enjoy them.

—Take "meditation breaks"—sit on a park bench, the beach, in a church, at the library, a quiet corner at home, permitting the healing power of silence to enter your mind, heart and soul.

—If you haven't allowed yourself to have a good cry—do so. When finished, wash your face and hands with cool water and go for a walk. It's wonderfully cleansing.

—To combat fatigue, eat a well-balanced diet, get plenty of rest, drink lots of water and have a regular exercise program.

If, however, you find yourself absolutely unable to carry off any of the above, you may be suffering from a much deeper form of depression.

Some symptoms of this affliction include feelings of despair, utter hopelessness, recurrent thoughts of death, extreme isolation, hostility, despondency, and withdrawal from life or contact with others.

Such severe depressive symptoms may require the attention of your doctor or a mental health professional, who may prescribe medication for you. Do not hesitate to seek help when needed.

*Walk placidly amid the noise and the haste—*
*be at peace in your world. You are a Child of*
*the Universe—you have a right to be here.*

—Desiderata

# 34

# Alcohol and Youth: A Deadly Mixture!

Alcohol and youth—a "deadly mixture" indeed, quite literally! Alcohol is the leading killer of our youth today. Tens of thousands of our young people between the ages of 16 and 24 die each year in alcohol related incidents.

That doesn't include the thousands more who suffer permanent life-long disabilities which result from these unfortunate occurrences.

Some studies have shown that 46 percent of teen suicide victims had been drinking before the suicide or suicide attempt. Drinking is also implicated in a high percentage of teen-age violence and crime. These are dire statistics! We must act to save our youth.

Alcohol is the number one drug of choice for the young, often beginning very young—as low as 8 or 9 years old. It is easy to get. Kids are often introduced to it by their parents, either directly or indirectly in the home. Maybe some of us don't know (or care) that alcohol is a drug which affects the central nervous system. It impairs judgment, coordination, behavior and can lead to life-long addiction. It is a "gateway drug"—often preceding the use of other drugs.

Alcoholism is defined as a "chronic, progressive and potentially fatal disease characterized by physical dependence on alcohol and/or damage to the brain, liver, or other parts of the body." It is repeated out-of-control drinking which also creates havoc in one's personal life, disrupts family life as well as social and professional life.

The disease can be arrested only through complete abstinence. With abstinence and good health care most people can recover from the physical and psychological damage caused by excessive drinking.

The solution to the ever-growing problem of teenage alcoholism lies with parents, relatives, teachers, therapists, youth ministers, clergy, athletic coaches—in fact, all of the adult community.

## Some ways in which parents and the community can help:

—Obtain accurate information about alcohol and its effects. "Under the Influence," by Dr. James Milan is an excellent resource describing the physiological affects of alcohol and alcohol addiction.

—Talk to youngsters in your care about the affects of alcohol.

—Do what you can to enhance their self-esteem and to assist them to set achievable goals.

—Provide and model a good value system and spiritual direction that will assist them in making intelligent choices about drinking and to become aware of the possible consequences of inappropriate choices.

—**Provide adequate supervision.**

—**Help them learn to resist peer-pressure and assume personal responsibility for themselves and their behavior.**

—**Provide wholesome recreational opportunities.**

—**Believe in them, love them and let them know it.**

How can you detect if your youngster is experimenting with alcohol? Following are a few signs or symptoms:

—**Sleepiness at unusual times.**

—**Sudden drop in grades, or erratic schoolwork.**

—**Extreme moodiness or mood swings.**

—**Change in behavior.**

—**Change in friendships and companions.**

—**Unexplained depletion of liquor supply in the home.**

If you suspect your child may be heading for trouble, get help! Talk to your physician, your minister or priest, the school, get counseling, take them to AA Meetings. Check out your community resources. Children and teenagers want and need to know that the adults in their lives care enough to do something about the problem. They desperately need the necessary structure and discipline even though they may rebel against it. Without it they have no sense of the boundaries and limitations necessary to become responsible citizens.

Children learn to behave more responsibly if they observe their parents and adults setting their own limits and boundaries. Above all, parents need to beware of the influence of their own behavior—the examples they set for their children.

*As the twig is bent—so grows the tree.*

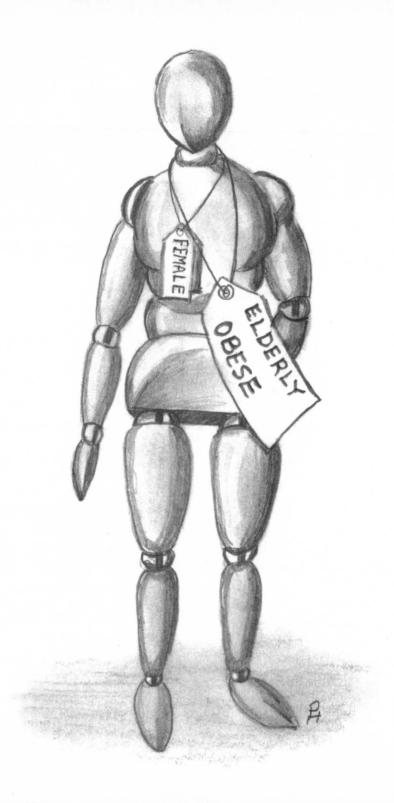

## 35

# Don't Let Others' Labels Define You

So often much of our self-image, good or bad, depends on what others think of us, how they perceive us.

That became quite apparent to me recently after a visit to my doctor's office. He referred me to a specialist and gave me my medical records to take to the new doctor. Well, I read them, much to my chagrin!

The "medical description" of me was, "An elderly Caucasian female, moderately obese." Ouch! That's not how I see myself! I know I am inching dangerously close to the big "7-0" but does that make me "elderly?" I don't even remember being middle-aged—how and when did I get to be "elderly"? I also know I'm carrying a few too many pounds on my bodily frame, but "obese"? even "moderately"? Couldn't he have said something kinder and gentler like "pleasantly plump?" I inwardly fussed about that for a while—objected even to be called "female" when the word, "woman" sounds so much nicer. I elaborated on the description in my mind, "A fat old female." Is that how people see me? How simply awful! Maybe I should wear a burlap bag over my head!

I ruminated on and on, then remembered words I've said to my clients thousands of times: "Watch your thoughts! Thoughts fuel feelings and feelings fuel thoughts"—and I decided to take my own counsel or I'd head into a full-fledged depression. The more I thought about it, the funnier it got. I've shared this with family and friends and have had many a laugh over it. When I told my daughters, they both shrieked into the phone (daughters are wonderful—so affirming), "What! How awful! Mom, you aren't elderly at all. I hope I look as good when I get to your age!" And "You're not obese—you are only..." (They didn't finish the sentence, bless their hearts—especially since they are both "twigs.")

Then I had dinner with a friend. I could tell by the glint in his eye I'd made a Big Mistake by telling him. I'd never hear the end of it! During dinner I was talking about an exciting "Elder Hostel" trip I'd like to take and he says, "Hmm—there seems to be a discrepancy here. It's OK to want to go on an Elder Hostel excursion but not OK to be called elderly?" (No comment from my side of the table!) Then, later as we paused in front of a store window, I was admiring a gorgeous outfit on a "toothpick" mannequin—he says, "Yes, it is beautiful—but would it look like that on a 'moderately obese female?'" I hit him, right there on the street—in front of God and everybody!

We all need to learn to become comfortable in our own skins no matter what our age or physical condition. Never allow other people's labels or opinions of you to define who or what you are. Be your own person. Even the young whipper-snappers of today will be elderly someday (if they live long enough). Learn to laugh at yourself—see the humor in things and events. Look at aging as only a small "pebble in your path not a major stumbling stone."

***For age is opportunity no less than youth itself.***

—Henry Wadsworth Longfellow

## 36

# The Case of the Invisible Woman

Have you ever felt invisible? You know, people just don't acknowledge your presence—don't notice you? You look down at your hands—they're there, you can see them—so the rest of you must be visible too—but it certainly doesn't seem so. Several of my friends have confided that they've had similar experiences.

What do these friends and I have in common? Why would we experience this same weird phenomenon? Well let me tell you—we are those who are viewed by those who should know better as "elderly women"—defined by the dreaded "E-word!"

I recently went into an electronics and computer store shopping for a new printer. Before I stepped through the door, I saw several salespeople standing around, but as I walked in they all disappeared like cockroaches into the woodwork when the light's turned on!

I walked through the store, stopped to look at printers, but no one came forward to help me. Several were gathered around a young man trying to help him find the right components to put a speaker system into his shower! Not one would even meet my eye. It was as though I wasn't there—as though I was totally invisible. I shook the "dust off my feet" and left.

Now if this were an isolated event I wouldn't be making a fuss about it. But as I asked around, it became apparent that this happens often to older women—especially in hardware stores, computer stores, large department stores, auto parts stores, and even in restaurants. Perhaps they think we are too ignorant or computer illiterate to know what we want? Or that anyone past 45 is senile and not to be taken seriously?

A friend and I were seated at a table in a restaurant. The waitress walked right by us several times as she waited on others—men, younger people, couples. My friend finally spoke up and said, "Excuse me, but are we invisible?" It got her attention. She seemed genuinely surprised as though she actually hadn't seen us. Another woman, after being ignored in an auto parts store, went out to her car, wrote what she wanted on a piece of paper, went back inside, and said, "My husband sent me here to get these parts," waving the piece of paper in the air. She was helped immediately!

Maybe women of my generation were taught to be "nice and polite" and to "wait our turn"—not to make waves or draw attention to ourselves. Well, maybe it's time for a little rebellion on our part! Isn't our money just as good at the bank? I don't suggest that we become surly, aggressive, or demanding but we must become more assertive, speak up and no longer tolerate this type of discrimination.

If that doesn't work, "shake the dust off your sandals," quit the premises, and take your business elsewhere.

Don't let the "E-word" get you down. Let it become a power word. There is power in a little quiet, determined, assertive rebellion. We must arise, flex our muscles and let ourselves be seen and heard. The wonders of this world are for all of us—not just the young. Aging is only a small "pebble" on the path of life—let's blithely walk along the path and not stumble as though it were a huge stone to trip over. After all in some cultures the "elders" are the most respected members of the community.

P.S. After this article was published in my newspaper column, I was approached by several older men saying women weren't the only "invisible ones"—they'd experienced the same treatment. A reader wrote saying that a young salesman had actually spoken to her in "baby talk." (At first she'd thought he had a speech impediment.) The problem must be much more widespread than I had originally suspected. All of us, younger or older, must act to end this discrimination against the older population. We are "either part of the problem or part of the solution." (Eldridge Cleaver)

Perhaps we all need to look at aging with a different pair of glasses, as someone said "It's better than the alternative." Perhaps we should say as Antoine de Saint-Exuptry said in "The little Prince"...

*It is only with the heart that one can see*
*rightly.*

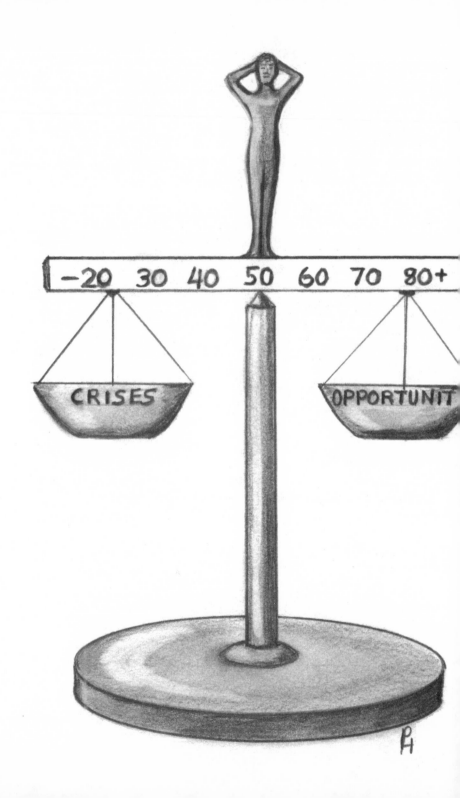

## 37

# Midlife Crisis?—or Opportunity?

Sometime between our fortieth and fiftieth birthdays we wake up to the fact that life is half over. If this awareness throws us into a panic, we can find ourselves in the throes of a painful "mid-life crisis."

In order to avoid the fear and pain involved in this time of life, people may try to run back into the past. They try to relive or regain their youth and sometimes behave as perpetual adolescents.

Mid-life is not so much a time of crisis as it is a time of "passage." It is a passage we all must walk through as we complete the tasks of the first half of life—those of growing up, establishing our families and our careers, etc. It is a time when we can look at our dreams and at how well we've done at reaching or achieving those dreams. Often we may feel that we've fallen short, that time is running out and we'll never make it. Disillusionment or despair may set in. We fear the unknown because we don't know how to control what the future holds for us.

However, everything has two sides, and on the other side of crisis lies opportunity if we will just look for it. We are much wiser in the second half of life with much more life experience and are more able to cope with life's challenges. What is there to fear? Maybe nothing so much as fear itself!

What are the opportunities of mid-life and beyond? You name it—the sky is the limit! Take out those old dreams and dust them off. Are they the same, or do they need some revision? Listen to what your heart says. "You should carefully observe the way toward which your heart draws you, then choose this way with all your strength." (Martin Buber)

Finding the "way of the heart" may take a little work. First, make peace with your past; forgive yourself for any failures and shortcomings of your youth. Forgive all who may have hurt you in any way. Hanging on to such memories places a wall around your heart and hinders progress.

Second, take your time. Be attentive to inner feelings and inspirations. By doing so, you'll know when it's time to take some action. Spend time by yourself; the second half of life demands time to reorient oneself.

Third, get reacquainted with your Self and ask some questions: what are your resources? your weaknesses? your blessings? your achievements? Become comfortable with who you are.

Fourth, be open to any new directions your heart and your Self may be leading you. You may find yourself with a startling change in your outlook on life, changes in your belief or value system, and physical changes as you age.

Take your time, do not act in haste. Look at this time of life—not as a time of crisis, but as a time of passage into a new land of opportunity. The best is yet to be.

> ***The second half of life is that for which the
> first was made."***
>
> —Carl Jung

## 38

# Some Thoughts on Retirement

They say there are two things we can do nothing about—death and taxes. I'd like to add a third—retirement.

Whether we like it or not, there comes a time when we have to leave the field of work either by choice, because of poor health, or because of company retirement policies.

For most people this is a sort of "mixed bag." On one hand they may look forward to it with a sense of excitement, while on the other hand there may be some fear and trepidation involved. Often they feel both scared and excited at the same time. Fear and excitement are opposite sides of the same coin. When fear is prominent, flip the coin and move on into excitement. It's a lot more fun.

"To retire" literally means to "withdraw from." Retirement means that now you choose what you want to withdraw from, such as the early morning alarm clock, punching the time clock, putting up with the daily grind of making deadlines, or having to be productive. You also get to choose what you want to move toward.

Retirement is only a change of proportions—a change in how you prioritize or use your time. Before I retired I did a lot of counseling, a little writing, and some teaching. Now I do a lot of writing, more teaching, and a little counseling. It's not a radical change, but I feel more in control of how I spend my time. Often, when retirees are asked how they spend their time, their response is, "I don't know how I ever had time to work!"

Looking forward to retirement can be like a much longed-for vacation. There's time for more travel than just the annual two- or three-week vacation. There's time to visit or re-visit the "old homestead"—back to beloved places, to reconnect with old friends and reminisce about the "good ole days." There's time to put your feet up and relax with a good book without guilt or feeling that you should be working or being more productive. There's time now to take up with whatever turns you on—new hobbies such as painting, gardening, reading just for fun. Above all, there's more time to spend with family and grandchildren.

At first it may be difficult to "let go." Sometimes there's a feeling of aimlessness, or of just drifting along without much purpose, which may bring on depression. Choose how you are going to spend each day. If it's to do nothing—to just "veg out"—great! But choose to do so, don't just let it happen aimlessly. You'll enjoy it much more and you'll feel that the day went just as you wanted it to—it didn't just fritter away.

Retirement gives you permission to be your own person and less accountable to others. My daughter said to me one day, "I can't wait to be your age." Surprised, I asked, "What on earth for? What's wrong with being your own age?" She quipped, "Because you can get away with more than I can." I asked if that meant I was eccentric or something. She didn't answer—just smiled sweetly and left me dangling!

Yes, you have the freedom to be as eccentric as you please as long it doesn't infringe on the rights and freedom of others.

Life consists of series of changes and new developments. Our mental attitude colors the quality of those changes and developments. As our body ages, we need to slow down, to enjoy the present moment more fully, to flow with the river of time and not buck the current by trying to swim upstream. (That doesn't get us anywhere—just tired and worn out.) Retirement is a time to withdraw from what you don't want and draw near to what you do want. It represents the ending of one phase of life and the brand-new beginning of another. The best years still lie ahead waiting for us to catch up with them.

## 39

# Does Your Vote Count?

On every Election Day, voter apathy is a major national concern. People are heard saying, "Why bother? What difference does it make? My vote doesn't count for much anyway!" Wrong! It counts, perhaps more than you can possibly imagine.

Every period in history has had its special challenges and those that face us as we draw nearer to a new century are as momentous as any in the past. The past hundred years have been marked by unprecedented advances in education, technology, medicine, agriculture, care of the environment, etc. It has also been marked by unspeakable atrocities, by brutal attacks of humanity against humanity in two World Wars; in smaller but not less intensely cruel wars between nations, ethnic cleansing within nations; terrorism, increase in crime and drug traffic, etc. What will the next hundred years hold for our children's children? It will surely be far different from yours or mine.

In his 1948 Inaugural Address, Harry Truman said, "The American people stand firm in the faith which has inspired this Nation from the beginning. We believe that all have the right to equal justice under the law and equal opportunity to share the common good. We believe that all have the right to freedom of thought and expression. We believe that all are created in the image of God. From this faith we will not be moved."

"The American people desire, and are determined to work, for a world in which all nations are free to govern themselves as they see fit and to achieve a decent and satisfying life. Above all else, our people desire, and are determined to work for, peace on earth, a just and lasting peace based on genuine agreement freely arrived at by equals. The supreme need of our time is to live together in peace and harmony."

He went on to describe democracy: "Democracy is based on the conviction that man has the moral and intellectual capacity as well as the inalienable right to govern himself with reason and justice. Democracy maintains that government is established for the benefit of the individual and is charged with the responsibility of protecting the rights of the individual and his freedom in the exercise of his abilities. Democracy has proved that social justice can be achieved through peaceful change. Democracy holds that free nations can settle differences justly and maintain lasting peace.

"Only by helping the least fortunate of its members to help themselves can the human family achieve the decent satisfying life that is the right of all people."

Truman's words are still viable today, half a century or more years later. They should be brought out and dusted off in any election year. They address issues such as the role of government in people's lives, welfare reform, the principle of equality and justice for all. Our former President has described the role of Democracy and its impact on our individual as well as in our collective lives.

In order to create a better life for all in the next hundred years, in order to take advantage of all the wonderful technologies humanity has attained, and in order to halt the atrocities against our fellow humans, we must all become involved. We must become informed and accountable and hold our political leaders' "feet to the fire." After all, this country is supposed to be a "government of the people, for the people, by the people."

The apathetic citizen may say, "So? That's all well and good. But still, what real difference would my one little vote make?"

Consider the following: (by George Herbert)

*"For want of a nail, the shoe is lost. For want of a shoe, the horse is lost. For want of a horse, the rider is lost. For want of a rider, the battle is lost. For want of a battle the war is lost."*

Your vote may be that nail.

# 40

# Where, Oh Where, Are the Green Pastures?

I received a birthday card which illustrated a fenced-off green pasture with a little old lady carrying a duffle bag and an umbrella, trying to climb the fence. The caption read, "The trouble with growing older is—by the time you have time to explore green pastures, you can't climb the darn fence!" True?

Well, maybe yes and maybe no. It depends on how we define "fences" and "green pastures." A fence may serve two purposes. It can be a protective border around a lush green pasture, protect us and give us a sense of security or it can become a restrictive barren desert—a barrier to growth and freedom—a prison of our own making.

What are some of our "fences" as we go through life? Three come to mind almost immediately—finances, health, and relationships. The primary "fence-builder" is attitude. All three of the above categories could become either green pastures or barren deserts depending on our attitude.

Take finances, for instance. Whether we are rich or poor, money can be either a blessing or a curse. We can be so wealthy that we are constantly afraid that someone will rob us, cheat us, or injure us trying to get at it. We can be so poor that we are always envious, jealous and fear there will never be enough. Both are operating from a concept of "lack." A prevailing attitude of "lack consciousness" is a definite barrier to entering into a peaceful and serene green pasture.

Much of our quality of life depends on our health, but even more than on the condition of our health, it is dependent on our attitude about our health. We all know people whose physical well-being is very poor or who suffer from severe disabilities but live lives far richer and more productive than others do who are in robust good health.

The loss of a primary relationship either through death or divorce can be a high fence to climb over. Life may indeed seem like a barren desert when we lose a child, a parent or other loved ones. If we can remember that "even as we walk through the valley of the shadow of death" we will know we will be lead once again to the "green pasture." If we can nourish and care for all the relationships we enjoy in the present, they will never be truly lost to us—we will always carry them in our minds and hearts.

Attitude and faith create and sustain the quality of life. No matter how tall the fence that we must scale—be it finances, health or relationships—a positive, upbeat attitude and deep abiding faith will help us clear it. We may not be able to bring in lots more money; we may not be able to cure a terminal illness; we may not be able to bring back a lost loved one; but we can still search for and find a "green pasture" where we can find happiness and fulfillment.

What and where might this be? It depends. It is different for everyone, and it may make take a little while for each person to figure out what this might be. All we ever really have is the present moment. No matter how good or how bad the past was we don't live there anymore. We can't live in the future either for it isn't here yet! Today is all there is.

I am reminded of the special green pastures my father set apart on his land. It was seeded and planted with wonderful lush grasses, a much deeper green than the rest of the fields. How contentedly the cows grazed there. They loved it—a place set apart. They didn't worry about yesterday or long for tomorrow. They just enjoyed today. It is just such a place we need—a place set apart where we can relax and just "be."

We don't need to travel to the far corners of the globe to find it. It can be a comfortable chair on your deck, a shaded spot in your garden, or a corner in your bedroom where you can read, listen to music, pray or meditate. Or it needn't be a physical "place" at all, but rather a quiet, serene "inner space"—a calm oasis where we can retreat in meditation—no matter what's going on around us.

Find that "green pasture," whatever that means to you, and I'll bet you won't even have to climb a fence to get there— you can just step into it.

*There is no cure for birth and death*

*save to enjoy the interval*

—George Santayana

# 41

# Is There Life After Birth?

Sometimes, as we ponder over the mystery of life, of birth, or of death, we may wonder—is there life after death? What do we really understand about either112?

Let me share a little story or legend I ran across some time ago concerning birth. Once upon a time, a pair of twins were growing and developing in their mother's womb. At first they felt very cozy and comfortable, warm, safe and secure as they swam around in the warm waters of their environment. But as they grew, they began to feel a little crowded and uncomfortable. They couldn't stretch out as they used to or to move around as freely. Still it felt warm, safe and secure. They decided they'd stay there forever, regardless.

Soon they heard voices talking about something called "birth" and wondered what that word meant. They began to pay attention and soon figured out that the word meant that they would have to leave the only world they knew. This frightened them. All sorts of questions began to plague them. "Is there life after birth? How will we move around? How will we get food?" They could find no answers to their questions and together they decided they would not leave, no matter what, it was too scary and unpredictable "out there."

One day a peculiar shoving began and they felt themselves being pushed through a long narrow hall and then—"out there"—into a huge, bright, empty space. The air felt cold, the lights too bright, and it was so noisy. They were so terrified they howled. However, soon they felt something warm wrapped around them. They were cuddled and held close. They then heard the same "thump-thump" beat of a soothing rhythm that was familiar to them. They also heard the same voice they'd heard many times before. They relaxed and drifted off to sleep, trusting and confident that there was indeed life after birth.

We may have the same questions about death. "Is there life after death? How will we move around?" Those who've had "near-death experiences" (NDE) report a long tunnel with a bright light at the end of it with a loving "Presence" there to greet them. They also report a place of beauty, peace, warmth and security—so wonderful that they were reluctant to return here. They, too, learned to trust that there is indeed "life after death."

I believe that life is eternal and that birth and death—the two portals of entry and exit into and out of this life—are simply two portals of entry and exit into and out of that wonderful journey called "life." Let us live it as fully and as happily as possible as we travel between those two doorways; and move forward with trust and confidence to whatever lies beyond; let each of us leave this planet a better place because we've passed through here.

# 42

# Can You Count Past a Hundred?

Let me begin with a little story from an old Asian tradition: Once there was a man who, after having looted a city, was selling his spoils—part of which were some priceless oriental rugs.

He'd go about the city shouting, "Who will give me a hundred pieces of gold for this rug?" A man stood by watching the transactions, then walked up to the "rug merchant" and asked, "Why are you selling these exquisite rugs for only a hundred pieces of gold?" The merchant, astonished, asked, "Is there any number higher than a hundred?"

In how many ways are we—you and I—like that rug merchant: not able "count past a hundred" or to see beyond our own perceived limitations?

Allow me to present a couple illustrations from my own life. I found myself, at age 42, divorced, with only a high school education and a few college credits, working as an office clerk at about $400 a month. My kid brother (twenty years my junior) had just finished college and was heading off to grad school. I was green with envy. I must have bemoaned this many times because one day he said, "I don't want to hear another word. In fact I'm sick of listening to you. Either get yourself up and off to college and do something about your life or quit whining about it!"

Well! I was affronted! That punk! How dare he say that to me! I'll show him! And though it took me many years, I did go back to school, eventually earned my graduate degree and entered the professional world.

Something which still turns me green with envy is to see someone on TV whizzing down a mountain skiing or gracefully gliding across an ice rink on skates. But I've had years of orthopedic surgery, and my left ankle is fused. It would break before it would bend. Now come on—even I know better! We've all heard about people with much worse afflictions. Those with only one leg who become accomplished skiers or champion athletes against unspeakable physical odds—not just one little fused ankle.

The point is I'm not willing to put forth the time and effort. I'm too afraid. I've convinced myself that I could never do it. I'd rather sit around, watch and whine, "If only..." It's a limitation I acknowledge and accept—knowing I'm not willing to do anything about it.

The only limitations we really have are those we acknowledge. The way we perceive ourselves and our capabilities, how we view the world of potential and possibilities are the determining factors of our quality of life.

While I was still pondering whether I could make it going back to college I said to a friend, "I don't know—I'll be past 50 by the time I get my graduate degree." She said "So? How old will you be if you don't?" I can't imagine what my life would have been if I had allowed my perception of aging to become a limitation.

Can you count past a hundred? Look at what you consider a limitation right in the eye. If it's one you can live with and still feel OK about your life—do so. If not—start counting 101, 102, 103...

Come on! Stretch—there's a whole new world out there.

# 43

# Creativity Is Ageless

Creativity is present within us as for as long as we draw breath into our lungs.

It begins in the curiosity of the infant; it is present in the constant exploration of the toddler; the inquisitiveness of the child continues on into adolescence, adulthood and well into old age if we allow this priceless gift to grow and flourish.

Creativity first takes hold in infancy when the baby is talked to, stimulated and exposed to a creative environment. The small child has a keen desire to explore his environment, to take things apart to see how they work, to try new combinations. Watch a child at play—you can almost see the wheels going around in their little minds.

They will view and value things so differently than adults. You may buy a child an expensive toy, give it to him with great anticipation of how much he will enjoy it—only to find he is much more interested in the box it came in!

How a child's creativity is responded to in childhood determines to a great degree how the adult will respond to inner creative impulses or urges. Parents and teachers can either encourage or suppress a child's creativity in their response to the child's curiosity or exploration in making unrealistic demands or in forcing a child into their own traditional mold. Parents often want their children to follow in their own footsteps and are dismayed or disappointed when the child wants to go in a different direction.

There are many ways a child's creative spirit can be nurtured in childhood. Kids don't need to be taught to be creative—they come that way! But often their native creativity dies due to lack of encouragement, by ridicule, or by a lack of opportunity to explore or develop their talents. Their creative potential may never be developed because of too much pressure and control—a drawing of a tree should "look" like a real tree, etc.

Children's creativity can also be stifled by their parents' busy schedules. There never is enough time to play, to daydream. They are hurried through childhood—at what cost we may never know. They are told to quit their "make believe," to "get real!" Of course there needs be a healthy balance between reality and fantasy, but if there's space for each, genius can flourish. Sometimes it's hard to tell which is which, but that is the wonder of childhood. When things are done just for the joy of it, creativity flourishes!

I remember as a little girl on the farm, I loved to watch Mom make pies, cakes and cookies. One day after watching her, I decided to make my own mud cookies just like hers. So I went into the chicken coop, got some eggs, mixed them up with mud and water, having a wonderful time squishing them with my little fingers.

I even decorated the tops with flower petals and put them in the sun to bake. They were beautiful. Well! Mom did not appreciate my creativity at all. I got a good scolding about being wasteful. My baking career ended right there. Who knows, I might have become another Betty Crocker or something, but I lost interest, didn't learn to cook or bake until after I married.

I'm not saying I should have been allowed to waste eggs making mud cookies, but I could have been encouraged to "help" in the kitchen and derived even more pleasure out of creating "real cookies" instead of make-believe ones. In my Germanic upbringing, creativity wasn't fostered—there wasn't time for "pretend stuff." "Life is real and life is earnest!" A family rule was "You can't go out and play til all the work is done."

Well, guess what? The work is never done! There is always more waiting.

Another motto was, "The devil finds work for idle hands." So, even to this day, I have a difficult time with leisure. I feel guilty even reading for pleasure (for work it's OK) when there are weeds in the garden and laundry to be done.

When things are done for the sheer joy of it, creativity flourishes. The more creative our children's learning environment is, the easier it is for them to learn. We must give ourselves and our children permission to enjoy learning—to do something for the fun of it—rather than "having to get it right" the first time. We must accept the premise that the pleasure of achievement is more important than the achievement itself.

Often parents drag their kids into the therapist's office because they are failing in school, refuse to do their homework, are being rebellious, etc. Many times the problem is that the kids are bored or overwhelmed with rules and work. Learning is something a child does naturally if it's fun, stimulating and they can have some ownership over it.

To give children ownership over their learning process, give them some choices. Let them decide when they will do their homework (not if). Some may need to play and unwind after a hard day at school and tackle the homework after dinner. Others would rather get it over with right away in order to have free time later. Still others would do better to get up earlier the next morning and do the work. Sometimes they may want to vary it to suit different occasions. What does it matter—as long as it gets done? We all feel better when we have some control over how we manage our time at home, at work or at play. Why would it be different for kids?

Creativity springs forth from the inner resources we have within us in great abundance, if we only believe that and allow it to surface. The secret here is "to allow." Creativity cannot be forced, pressured, or produced on demand. It has to be allowed to flow. This means having the time, the space, and the opportunity for the creative juices to bubble up into consciousness and to flow freely.

Creative people have a passion, a zest for whatever they do; a real capacity for enjoyment because they are in tune with their inner selves. What may appear to others to be extremely hard work and pressure, they will regard as "pleasure not pressure" for they are only doing "what comes naturally."

We are all born with great potential for creativity beyond our wildest imagination. You may scoff and say, "Oh, yeah? Not me! I don't have a creative bone in my body." Not so! The creative urge is what kept you going when you were learning to walk, and all you did for a while is fall on your bottom. The creative urge was there when you were learning to talk, couldn't get the words out right, and got frustrated because people couldn't understand you. But you persisted until you could and they did. It's natural and normal to want to do bigger and better things, to grow and to learn.

So what happens along the way? Somewhere we began to be afraid of non-acceptance, ridicule, failure, criticism, blame, or punishment. We we no longer make "mud cookies" and aren't interested in making "real cookies." An inner voice awakens, a "judgmental voice" that is far more damning and daunting than any external voice could ever be. This voice (or judgmental self) makes us afraid to try anything creative or innovative, then chides us because we didn't—especially if someone else gets the idea and carries it out successfully. This judgmental self derides us when we do something and derides us again when we don't.

There is a constant battle between the creative self we were born with and our judgmental self. The creative self says, "You can." Our judgmental self says, "You can't—just who do you think you are?!" And so the battle within rages and the creative self often loses out.

In order to win this battle, we need to silence the judgmental self and its strong voice. We need to look at and understand its source. Some of it comes from childhood conditioning; some from the culture we live in—its social structure and the taboos within that structure. Some of it comes from outgrown religious beliefs we no longer hold consciously but that still influence us unconsciously.

We all have "barriers to creativity" that inhibit or destroy the God-given creativity and talents with which each of us is born. We need to identify what these are, eliminate them and move ahead.

Before we can make that identification, we need to become aware. Awareness is the first step in silencing the voice of the judgmental self and allowing the voice of the creative self to speak out. As the creative voice is given free reign it brings with it another gift—that of critical evaluation.

Critical evaluation may give us the same basic message or information that the judgmental voice gives but the "tone" is entirely different. It doesn't hand down the verdict—"That's stupid and so are you," "That wouldn't work in a hundred years," or similar statements.

Critical evaluation would be more like, "That might not work, but try this." Critical evaluation does not instill fear, anxiety or stifle our creative endeavors. It is curiosity based—not fear based; it encourages spontaneity, freedom, risk-taking and prods us on to achieve our goals and desires. Critical evaluation can also serve as the "voice of conscience" in helping us to make sound moral choices.

Creativity barriers have been "alive and well" for eons. Who knows what has not been tried or achieved because of them?

Consider the following: A banker once advised a potential investor in the Ford Motor Company not to invest because, "The horse is here to stay, the automobile is just a fad." In 1946, D.F. Zanuck commented, "Video won't be able to hold on to any market for longer than six months. People will soon get tired of staring at a plywood box every night." The congressman who suggested in the late 1800s that the US Patent Office be closed, because everything that could possibly be invented has been invented. Imagine how different life would be if those creativity barriers had prevailed.

You may be thinking, "But those are big-league items, I could never come up with any ideas that great." Consider the story of a 13-year old who loved to ice skate. He hated to wear a hat but also couldn't stand to have his ears cold. So together with his grandmother, they took some padding and some wire and fixed a contraption that fit over his head, covered his ears and kept them warm so he could skate in comfort. The other kids laughed at him at first, but soon they too wanted some "ear muffs" to keep their ears warm. Think of the a "yo-yo," the "hoola-hoop," or even the "pet rock." Who would have imagined taking a small rock painting a face on it—two eyes, a nose and a mouth—and selling it for six dollars?

Guess who's laughing all the way to the bank?

Fostering creativity in ourselves and in our children is vital if we are ever to create a "new world order." We must dream the "what ifs" and allow ourselves to become "possibility thinkers." We must "dream the impossible dream"—allow time and space for exploration, for play, for making mistakes. Things don't need to be perfect, but they do need to be fun!

Allow your creative self to emerge and your creative voice to speak. Dare to be positive in the face of negativity, allow the spirit of optimism to grow and flourish, value your intuition and your gut reactions and grant yourself permission to take risks and make mistakes. Challenge yourself to think and do things differently.

*If you always do what you've always done,*
*you'll always get what you always got.*
*You'll always do what you've always done,*
*if you always think what you've always thought.*

—Larry Wilson, Pecos Learning Center

# 44

# The Significance of Dreams

Though we may not always remember, we dream every night. In fact, dream researchers and experts claim that we dream several times a night—at least four or five different dreams.

Your dreams can enhance your life and give you new insights into old problems or new ideas—from simple projects to complex inventions. History is full of stories about inventors, writers, artists and musical composers who credit their dreams for much of their creativity.

However, much of the time our dreams don't make any sense to us. It could be because we don't understand "dream language," which is a language of symbols and metaphors. It's like visiting a foreign country and trying to communicate without knowing the language, or, when entering the world of computers, having to learn "computerese," a new and different language with its own vocabulary.

So it is with dreams. Their "messages" come to us from the subconscious mind, using a language of symbols and metaphors we need to understand before we can decode these messages. Yet it is far more complex than just learning the vocabulary and grammar of a new language. Vocabulary and rules of grammar can be cut and dried; if you know them, you know them. Not so with dream language.

Each of us is unique; each of us can come up with a different interpretation for the same dream symbol, and each of us will be right! Dreaming about a cat, for instance, may have a different meaning for different people, depending on whether they are fond of cats, terrified of cats, or very allergic to them. And, a dream about cats may not really be about cats at all, but a symbolic message from yourself to you.

Very seldom should dreams be taken literally. Let me share a "cat dream" with you to illustrate my point: I dreamed that my cat was coming toward the door on the deck, drenched to the skin from pouring rain, looking so exhausted he could barely put one paw in front of the other, and his "meow" was barely audible. I brought him in, wrapped him in a blanket, dried him, rocked him and crooned to him softly. He relaxed, his fur became soft and fluffy and he began to purr loudly. As I continued to hold him, I was thinking, "You poor, stupid cat! You have your own cat-door; you didn't have to stay out there in the cold, pouring rain. You don't even have sense enough to come in out of the rain!" I woke up.

Now it doesn't take much analysis to see what that dream was trying to tell me. "Who doesn't have sense enough to come in out of the rain?" I often overextend myself until I'm exhausted and feel I can't put one foot in front of the other. Perhaps, I too, need to wrap myself in a blanket, relax, purr, rest and sleep.

Our conscious mind shuts down during sleep, but the subconscious mind never does. It's on the job twenty-four hours a day, seven days a week. We all have our very own "built-in consultant," and we can ask for input from this consultant every night of the week. Why don't we use this vast source of information, knowledge and wisdom? Perhaps it's because we haven't learned to value the source.

We may wake up in the morning with the memory of a dream that is so bizarre we don't even want to look at it. It may be one that seems like pure nonsense, or one so "ordinary" you feel it's a waste of time to dwell on it; it couldn't possibly have any worthwhile meaning. However, if we look at every dream as important and take the time to study it, we'll find that even the "one-liners" have an important lesson to teach. We can learn much from an "ordinary" dream, maybe even more than from the bizarre or wild-fantasy kind.

In order to benefit from our "dream-life," however, we need to have good "dream-recall." If we don't remember our dreams they are as much good to us as an unread book sitting on the bookshelf.

We can teach ourselves to remember our dreams. It takes some effort and commitment but it is worth it. Following are some suggestions to help in dream recall.

## 1) Keep a dream journal

Get a special journal to be used only for recording dreams—preferably an unlined one. Sometimes it's helpful to draw some of your dream images, and lines may inhibit your drawing. Keep the journal and a pencil by your bedside.

## 2) Write it down

Upon awakening, jot down the date. If you remember a dream write it down immediately. Waiting for even a

few moments may cause the dream to slip away. If
you remember only little snippets of a dream write it
down. Doing so may help in recalling more details or
even total recall. Take note of your thoughts and
feelings upon awakening. Did you wake up feeling
happy about something but don't know why, feeling
sad, angry or confused? Write it down. If you find it
difficult to express in words, draw or sketch a
symbolic image of it. But do record it. This journal
will become a valuable, indispensable tool for
working with your dreams.

## 3) Ask for dreams

Before going to sleep, ask yourself for dreams to help
solve some problem or to give you new ideas or
information. This may take some practice and may not
work at first, but this kind of pre-sleep attention seems
to sort of "prime the pump." Keep at it and one day
you'll see—it works!

## 4) Look for symbolism

Don't be too quick with a literal interpretation of your
dream. They are often coded in symbolic language.
Look for symbols and ponder about what meaning
they have for you. Also look for a play on words, cli-
ches, puns—they often help clarify meanings.

## 5) Look for the deeper message

Assume that the dream is a message to you from a
deeper part of yourself—your subconscious mind. It

may be trying to tell you something you are only dimly aware of, feel deeply about, or are unwilling to admit to or face up to in your waking life.

## 6) Assume that all parts of the dream represent some aspect of yourself

Even when dreaming of someone else, or about some very unusual circumstances, assume that each element or part of the dream represents some aspect of yourself and what's going on in your life. This may sound confusing, but ask yourself some questions. "What does this remind me of?" "What's going on in my life that somehow feels similar to the feeling of this dream." If nothing makes any sense, ask for another dream to help clarify it.

Sometimes you'll have several dreams which seem totally unrelated.

But as you keep recording them in your journal you may notice a pattern or continuing theme which will help in understanding the dreams' message(s).

## 7) Don't give up

Even if you don't have a clue about what's going on with your dreams, or you keep having a hard time remembering them, write something in your journal every morning.

Even if it's just the date and a note—"Don't remember," write about your feelings and thoughts upon awakening. Be patient and persistent; you'll eventually get results.

There are many books on the market about dreams and their symbols. Some of the symbol-meanings may apply to your dreams, some may not; or they may apply one time and not the next. It depends on what they mean to you in the context of your own life. Only you can determine whether the symbolism "rings true" for you.

Following are some rather "generic" dream symbols and they hold true in a general way, but they must be applied in context to the "story" of your dream.

**House:** Your body, environment, sometimes your personality.

**Home:** Your basic security or insecurity depending on the dream content.

**Room:** Woman, womb. Dreaming of a set of rooms which never existed in your own home, usually means the beginning of a new endeavor or discovery.

**Car:** Movement of the body or life. Are you in the driver's seat or in the passenger's seat? Who is in control?

**Boat:** Security or insecurity. What's happening—is the boat sailing safely or in danger of sinking? Is the water calm or stormy?

**Lifeboat:** Reassurance. You won't "drown" in your problem(s).

**Water:** Emotions, intuition, activity of the subconscious mind.

**Fire**: Energy, enthusiasm. Also danger and challenges. A dream of a campfire usually represents reassurance or inner contentment.

**Snakes:** Phallic symbol, sex or fear of sex; temptation.

**Serpent:** Wisdom or knowledge.

**Flying:** Wish for freedom or release. Achievement or accomplishment.

**Locks:** Inhibitions or restrictions. Are you "locked in or out" of an area of your life?" Also a female sexual symbol.

**Key:** The resolution to a problem; key to someone's heart.

**Losing keys:** Frustrations or lack of attentiveness in some area of life.

**Birth:** Beginning of something new, new ideas, new start in life.

**Child:** Innocence, symbol of the future, a developing idea or concept; may be an immature aspect of self.

**Death**: The ending of something, change, transformation.

**Coffin:** Laying something to rest; coming to terms with something, or a greater need of freedom of expression.

**Funeral:** Death or end of something, a project ending, or a readiness for something new or different.

**Lightning:** Sudden revelation; symbol of an innovative, new idea.

**Animals:** Pets—love and affection. Wild animals—fear insecurity or panic. Hunting animals—search for something such as excitement, perfection, etc.

**Monster:** Something greatly feared. Some aspect of self or life.

**Nudity or nakedness:** Several meanings: "Bare facts"—the undisguised truth. Clothes may need attention; you feel exposed or vulnerable in some area of your life; you are seeking attention from the opposite sex.

**Work:** Mission, purpose, or potential in life.

**Fog:** Not seeing things too clearly.

**Fence:** Feeling "fenced in," restricted, limited, prevented from doing something you really want to.

**Worry:** Unconscious doubts or fears; reveals areas of life you may feel unsure about or which may need your attention.

**Pursuit:** If you are being pursued, think about what or who is chasing you. Is there something you wish to escape from? If you are doing the pursuing—what are you chasing after in your waking life? Is there something you want to "catch up to" or just "catch?"

The above is only a thumbnail sketch of common dream symbols. The list could go on for many pages. These are some of the most commonly interpreted meanings, but they need to be developed further in view of a particular dream and with what's going on in the dreamer's everyday waking life.

As you become more aware of the significance of dreams, more able to recall them, and are keeping a dream journal, you'll be able to "read" or interpret these messages from your subconscious mind—your inner self.

Never jump too quickly into a literal interpretation of a dream. A dream about a terrible quarrel with a loved one may signify that different aspects of yourself are at war with each other. On one hand you may want to do this, on the other hand you might want to do that and can't up make your mind. You feel at odds with yourself. Your subconscious mind may be telling you to get your act together and quit the internal fighting. And, perhaps act a little more loving toward yourself. Dreaming of the death of someone close to you needn't throw you into a panic thinking someone is going to die. Death dreams usually mean the end of something and the beginning of something new.

Never take a dream out of context with what's going on with your life. Dreams do not happen in isolation—they relate to what's happening in your own unique situation. Sometimes they seem too far-fetched and it's hard to make any connection. Keep looking. At times the message is not very clear because consciously we may not want to see it or face it. Your dreams will send you the same message in several different "codes" until you finally "get it."

At other times you get such incredible "one-liners"— they really grab you with their message. Here's one. I was at odds with myself, wrestling with a problem. In my dream, I was asleep and a huge bear jumped on my bed. As I tried to sit up he bit off my nose.

I sat up in horror and (still in my dream) I heard the words, "You're biting off your nose to spite your face." I woke up—laughed and said OK I get the message." It was wonderful—problem solved.

Pay close attention to your feelings as you work with a dream because they give you clues to what's going on in your inner life and may be trying to get your attention in your waking life. What are the anxieties, fears, joys, elation, expectations or wishes that you are experiencing in your dreams. What do they remind you of? Keep notes in your journal.

Examine the people, animals, objects, actions and environments in your dreams. What do they mean to you and how do they affect you? What do their activities or participation remind you of in your daily life? How do they relate? Take your time with this and write it all out. All this writing may seem time consuming and sometimes it is, but it is indispensable in your dream work. Putting things down on paper helps clarify your thoughts and feelings, which in turn helps in the final understanding and comprehension of your dreams.

Remember, no one else can really interpret a dream for you. Other people and books may help, but ultimately only you know whether a particular interpretation feels right; whether it resonates with you and feels true.

Working with your dreams over a period of time does take some work and commitment, but it is really worth the effort.

Spending this much time working on your own psyche gets you in touch with your own inner self. You'll be surprised at the intuitive guidance which is right there within you, and become more intimately acquainted with you, yourself, and what makes you tick.

*Know thyself and thou knowest all things.*

# 45

# Laugh it Up! It's Good for You!

We all know how wonderful a good belly-laugh feels. You know, the rolling-on-the-floor, tears-streaming-down-your-face, clutching-your belly-til-it-hurts kind of laugh. It totally relaxes the innards, relieves tension and almost feels like a new lease on life. "Ooh—that was so wonderful" we say as soon as we can catch our breath.

Laughter has been called "the best medicine" and has been credited with curing serious illness. Normin Cousins, in his book, *An Anatomy of an Illness*, said that laughter helped him recover from a serious degenerative spinal condition. He had his hospital bed set up in a luxury hotel room, hired some nurses, (said it was cheaper than staying in the hospital), rented lots of comedy videos and laughed himself well. He called laughter "inner jogging." It is a beneficial inner exercise, for it increases the circulation, increases the intake of oxygen, reduces pain and inflammation and stimulates an alertness hormone which facilitates learning. Don't we always remember something better if it's connected with something humorous?

Laughter and humor can also help "grease the wheel" at the workplace. We need to loosen up, not take ourselves so seriously; that goes for both management and labor. We make a dumb mistake, and instantly it's Doomsville! Lighten up—no one is perfect, not even the boss! Admit the mistake, laugh at yourself, do what you can to correct it, then drop it. Even serious blunders can be worked through easier with a little levity.

A little joke or humor relaxes the atmosphere, resolves conflict, opens communication, boosts motivation and increases productivity.

What more could anyone want? And it's free! How does laughter improve productivity? It increases the intake of oxygen and oxygenates the blood, giving us more energy. Having more energy makes us more alert and more capable of interaction with fellow workers.

Humor also makes it easier to give or take negative feedback when it is necessary; it softens frustrations that are part of every working environment. Cartoons and posters can work wonders to lift the spirit.

Of course, not everything is a laughing matter. There are times when laughter and jokes are inappropriate. Tactless, distasteful or sarcastic jokes at the expense of others are always out of line. Jokes used to divert attention away from the business at hand can be counter-productive and irritating rather than funny.

But on the whole, laughter is not only good for our health, it is good for all our relationships, our careers, our spiritual lives. In fact it's good for our whole quality of life.

So lighten up, laugh, be happy! Become more playful, enjoy your family, remember funny stories to share with others. Laughter is contagious. Let someone catch yours.

As was seen on a bumper sticker: "She who laughs— lasts!"

# 46

# Have You Had Breakfast?

Have you, like so many people, grabbed a cup of coffee, maybe a piece of toast and bolted out the door this morning? According to nutritionists, breakfast should be the most nourishing and substantial meal of the day. In fact, we should "Eat like a king at breakfast, like a prince at lunch and like a pauper at dinner."

We wouldn't dream of taking off in the car on an empty tank, but that's exactly what we do to our bodies. The only reason it works as long as it does is that the body is so much more efficient than a car and can run longer on "empty." But it eventually runs dry!

Good nutrition is not only of vital importance in our physical health, but also in our mental and emotional health. We need adequate quantities of complex carbohydrates, vegetables, fruits, proteins and dairy products daily and a good portion of that should be consumed at breakfast.

The major problem rests with the "morning rush hour." I'm not referring to the traffic rush hour, but rather the "personal rush hour." If we could have a leisurely morning, eat a wholesome meal, linger over that second cup of coffee, tea or fruit juice, start the day at a less hectic pace, the digestive juices would flow easier; our stomach wouldn't knot up, the day would be off to a much better start, and almost certainly to a much better ending. It may take some planning, maybe getting to bed a little earlier and getting up a little earlier in order to have the extra time. But it is worth the effort.

Doing a morning's work on an empty stomach, not only brings about fatigue and less resistance to illness, it is also responsible for loss of mental and physical efficiency—causing more errors, mistakes and irritability—considerable loss of productivity.

Studies have proven that children who begin the school day with little or no breakfast have difficulty concentrating and being attentive, average poorer grades and get into more squabbles and fights. Generally, they do much poorer in school, academically, socially and physically than those who begin the day with a good breakfast under their belts.

An initial question I ask a client who is in acute emotional or mental stress is "How is your nutrition?" Invariably the answer is, "Lousy!"

I am continually appalled at the gross nutritional neglect people subject their bodies to and expect them to function well. Many times my "prescription" is a baked potato with cottage cheese for breakfast. It may sound like rather strange breakfast fare, but it works wonders. It begins the day with a good complex carbohydrate (the potato) which acts like a slow-release energy pill and adds potassium and Vitamin C. The cottage cheese provides protein and calcium. When cooked in the microwave, the potato is done in about six minutes, an easy way to begin experiencing the benefits of breakfast. Try it. Your body will thank you.

Remember, it's been about ten to twelve hours since you've had food. Food is a major source of energy, and this source is not inexhaustible—it needs to be replenished. The very word, breakfast, speaks for itself. It means "to break the fast"—ending the overnight fasting from food.

It may be difficult to begin a new morning routine for yourself and your family. You've become accustomed to rushing around like a headless chicken in the morning. But when you gradually begin to let go of that frantic pace you'll be able to really experience the enjoyment of sitting down to a good morning meal, dawdle over it, and begin the day on a relaxed and much happier note.

You'll be healthier, function better both mentally and physically, have more energy, feel happier and enjoy life more. Who knows? You might even feel like doing something fun in the evening with the family or friends instead of just being a couch potato in front of the TV! All of that from just eating breakfast? Isn't it worth a try?

Plan your meals as though your life depends on it—**it does!**

*Come what may, time and the hour run
through the roughest day.*

—William Shakespeare

47

# How to Find the Time You Never Knew You Had

We all waste a lot of time worrying about time.
There never seems to be enough of it to go around.
We wring our hands and wail, "I wish I had more
time to spend with my family or friends, or more
leisure time for the things I really want to do, but
there are only twenty-four hours in a day!" "If there
were forty-eight, it wouldn't be enough!"

Then there's the pressure to have not just time, but
"quality time." What does the term, "quality time," mean?
Does it mean special out-of-the-ordinary-time that we should
carve out of our already busy schedules, and then feel guilty
because we either don't or can't? Or could it include the very
"ordinariness" of life—the little ordinary daily activities? The
small thirty-second acts of love and tenderness; a whisper of a

kiss on the end of the nose, a gentle touch on the cheek, a soft smile from across the room—these are what fond memories are made of.

Quality time can be had by doing simple, ordinary chores together. A child standing on a stool helping with the dishes, can become a time of intimate sharing; talking about what's going on in his or her little mind and a time of sharing what's going on in yours. Doing homework, folding laundry or any other chores can serve a twofold purpose—that of getting things done and spending some good quality time together. Bedtime can become either a source of frustration with children resisting or it can become a beautiful way to end the day with a bedtime ritual of story-telling, night prayers and a comfy tucking in—real quality time.

We really do have all the time we need for anything we really want to do. It's a matter of setting priorities—a matter of taking a good look at how time is actually spent versus the way we think it ought to be spent.

Take a good look at how your time is used:

## A) Morning

Do you get up late, rush around edgy and irritable because time is running short? Might the day get off to a better start if you got up thirty minutes earlier; took the time for a second cup of coffee, played with the kids a bit; or relaxed and took time for meditation? It's the same thirty minutes, but it would add so much more to the day than just another thirty minutes in bed.

## B) Commuting to and from work

Whether you walk, take the bus, or drive to work, use that time well. Listen to books on tape, things you wish you had time to read; listen to calm, relaxing music to start your day in a relaxed frame of mind. If riding the bus, use the time to read, knit, or even nap.

## C) Coffee breaks and lunch hour

These are precious moments; relax and enjoy them. Sometimes the best way to use this time is to do absolutely nothing. Sit back, empty the mind, do some deep breathing and just stare at a spot on the wall. Relax and daydream. Often we can accomplish much more later if we will take some time out to just be.

## D) After work, evenings and weekends

Take a close look at how you spend those hours and minutes. Who do you spend them with? Do changes need to be made here and there? Don't wait until the kids are grown and then wish you'd spent more time with them.

Sometimes the deepest sorrow the bereaved feel is the regret over not giving their most valuable gift—that of time—to a lost loved one.

## E) Sleep

How much do we really need? There are many variations in peoples' need for sleep. Experiment to see how much you need to rest and recoup your energy level, then see that you get it, but no more than that. Getting up earlier or staying up later may bring you "quality time" you may not experience otherwise.

Allow your sleep time to work for you. The subconscious mind never sleeps and is able to work out solutions to problems while consciousness is at rest. Pose a question or problem to your subconscious mind just before going to sleep, and more often than not, the answer will be there in the morning upon awakening.

Being ever mindful of the present moment and savoring it goes a long way in granting us quality time, first with ourselves then with those we love. We may feel that not all our moments are "savor-able," but we can still be mindful of them and do what we can to transform them into something more to our liking. Quality time begins with peace within. An inner calm begets an outer calm which changes and enhances the immediate environment, bringing about a change in the quality of life.

There is a deep connectedness between a deep personal peace and the quality of the time we spend on our day to day activities—the ordinary, sometimes repetitive or boring aspects of life—which can be changed into something new, extraordinary and precious.

We have all the time we need; we just have to figure out where to look for it in our daily routine and decide how to consciously and deliberately use it to create a life touched with a peace, love and happiness.

Imagine yourself at the end of your life, reviewing how you have spent the "time of your life" and being able to say, "I found the time I needed and used it well."

## 48

# A Time for Thanksgiving

We have so much to be thankful for in this great land of ours. When you think of how young this country is—only a little over 220 years—it is truly amazing to contemplate—that all that has been accomplished has taken place is such a brief time in history.

The freedoms and opportunities, which we sometimes take for granted, are unparalleled in the world. Let's take the time on Thanksgiving Day to remember some of these and offer heartfelt prayer of thanks-giving.

—**For the gift of life and the opportunities and challenges our country offers to all its citizens.**

—**For our talents and abilities—that may we use them for the betterment of life.**

—**For our trials, weaknesses and mistakes—that we may learn from them.**

—**For the beauty that surrounds us—that we may see it and appreciate in ourselves, in others, in nature—wherever we find it.**

—For the gift of potential—the possibility of transcending past limitations and becoming all that we can be.

—For the gifts of freedoms—of speech, of worship, and of liberty for all.

—For our country with all of its successes and all of its failings—its dedication to "life, liberty and the pursuit of happiness."

—For our planet in all of her beauty and splendor—may we always cherish and protect Mother Earth—for the sake of our children and our children's children.

—For our families. Though many are torn asunder by death or divorce, let us acknowledge and give thanks for life, love and the unique opportunities for growth and development that good family life offers.

—For all the good times, and for forgiveness of self and others for the bad times.

—For peace. Though peace is not universal on our planet today, let us give thanks for where it does exist and do all we can to spread "peace on earth and good will toward all."

—For the gift of every new day—for another opportunity to live in a way to bring peace, joy, love and happiness to ourselves and others.

—For faith in God and the freedom of worship.

—For special blessings received—let us give thanks.

Take this list or make up one of your own and make it a part of your Thanksgiving Day celebration of "thanks-giving."

Let us all adopt "an attitude of gratitude" not just on our annual Thanksgiving Holiday, but as a way of life for all the days of our lives.

### *HAPPY THANKSGIVING TO ALL!*

# 49

# Advent: A Season for Hope

The fourth Sunday before Christmas ushers in the Season of Advent. The word, "advent," means "approach, forthcoming or drawing near." In the Christian Church, it marks the beginning of a new liturgical year and a looking forward to the celebration of Christmas—the birth of Jesus Christ.

Ideally, it should be a time of reflection about what this Holy Season is all about—a time to look at the meaning of life, the role love plays in our lives, the role of harmony, peace and good will to our families, communities, nation and the world at large; a time to reflect on what role we might be able to play to help bring "peace on earth."

Often we are far too busy to even pause a few moments for such reflections. Perhaps we are too busy with the wrong things leading to feelings of frustration, exhaustion, depression—the "holiday blues."

There is always the tug between good and evil, between despair and hope. This reminds me of a story about a Jewish Rabbi sitting in his study listening to a Christian friend trying to convert him to Christianity. His friend was earnestly trying to convince him that Christ had indeed come into the world and fulfilled the prophecies concerning the Messiah in the Old Testament, that Jesus was sprung from the "root of Jesse, born in Bethlehem, from the line of David...." The Rabbi said nothing—just listened quietly.

Then he got up went over to the window, flung it open and stood there looking out for a long time. He turned to his friend and asked, "Where IS your Messiah?" He was not looking for the Messiah to come walking down the street. He had thrown open the windows to the world—and what did he see? Violence, bloodshed, even in the very land where Jesus walked. Cain still murders his brother Abel. We have not yet "beat our swords into plowshares" or "our spears into pruning hooks" as Isaiah prophesied. We, as a people, do not yet walk, "In the light of the Lord."

Does that mean that the Messiah never came? No, I believe it means we have not really heard, or truly believe in our heart that He came. Oh, we may have heard the words, but only with our ears and not with our hearts. So we give in to despair, say that hope is an illusion; the world is a mess and that it is going to hell in a hand basket!

Maybe we succumb to feelings of despair at times because we don't take the time to value and enjoy life's gifts enough, such as loving families, loyal friendships, home, job, music, sunrise and sunsets, nature, good food, fresh water, clean air and above all the healing power of a faith in God. Are we really that busy? If we must answer that question in the affirmative, perhaps Advent is a time to begin to realize how precious life is—every single minute of every single day.

Yes, there is pain, sorrow, poverty, illness and death in this world, but we can learn to transcend those with faith, hope and love. Advent is a season of both darkness and light. Sometimes the tunnel of everyday life may seem dark, dreary and hopeless, but if we can learn to look up we'll see there's light at the end of that tunnel. That light is "The Light," the hope of mankind—born into our midst at Christmas.

Focusing on that light brings builds faith, brings hope, and increases the capacity to love. Reflect on the story of the Jewish girl who escaped the Nazis in Poland and hid in a cave. She died before she could be saved, but she left this message of hope on the wall in the cave: "I believe in the sun even when it is not shining, I believe in love even when not feeling it, I believe in God even when He is silent."

Let us not live in a "land of despair" but rather in a "land of hope" where we can still see the world's reality as it is—with all its problems and tragedies, but we can work to make it better. We can all work to improve it, beginning on a very small scale with just you and me.

As we continue on our advent journey—the "drawing near" to Christmas, let us remember "the reason for the season." Let it be a time of hope and anticipation.

***Let there be peace on earth and let it begin
with me.***

# 50

# The Ghost of Christmas Past (Why We Get the Holiday Blues)

The Holiday Season—from Thanksgiving to New Years—is an exciting, wonderful time for many. Yet for others it can be a time of great stress, anxiety, pain and grief—bringing on a poignant case of the "Holiday Blues."

Why such totally opposite reactions and responses? Our attitude toward Christmas depends a great deal on our own personal history, our culture and what our experience has been especially involving the celebration of Christmas. It also depends on our expectations—on what we think it "should be." Christmas, "past, present and future" somehow gets rolled up into one big emotional package of feelings that resurfaces year after year.

For many, the joyous singing of Christmas carols are grim reminders of a childhood of poverty, abuse, or neglect—of parents hurting them or too drunk to care about them and their Christmas, etc. Sadly, the cycle keeps repeating itself and today's parents, perhaps unknowingly, recreate the same scenario in their own adult lives and families. For others there is pain, anguish and feelings of failure at being unable to provide for their children as their parents had done for them. These deep feelings can be especially poignant during the Christmas season.

Christmas can be the loneliest time of the year. It often was for me on Christmas Eve after the kids went to bed. My husband had begun his "celebrating" early and was snoring on the couch. It was such a lonely feeling playing "Santa" by myself. It could have been so wonderful. Instead I went quietly about putting things under the tree with tears running down my face—quietly so I wouldn't wake him or them. I never experienced a lonelier time in my life!

That is part of my Christmas memory bank. Though that was many years ago, the feelings connected with that time pop to the surface of my consciousness. I experience those same feelings all over again, bringing with them the tears (even as I am writing this). If I allowed myself to dwell on this, I could come down with a good case of the "blues."

Remember always that "thoughts fuel feelings and feelings fuel thoughts," and that what we allow our minds to dwell on creates our reality. I could dwell on those old memories and become desperately lonely even amidst family and friends. Or, I can let go of those thoughts, recall the good times or create new experiences and not be lonely at all—to feel peace and joy in solitude even when I spend Christmas Eve alone.

Somehow as Christmas approaches our hopes and expectations soar. Maybe—just maybe—things will be better this year. At the same time we may become fearful because maybe they won't! And so fear wins over optimism.

To overcome this, take a long objective look at what your observance of Christmas has been. We all have certain rituals around holidays unique to our own families. Examine yours. What has real meaning for you now, today, and what is merely an empty rite which no longer nourishes your spirit.

Look for meaning. Christmas is essentially a religious Feast Day, not a secular holiday like the Fourth of July. Maybe that is what is missing—a longing for connectedness with something or Someone beyond one's self. So often I've heard people say, "I have to get back to basics," and when asked just what that means, it translates into a search for God, for faith (perhaps put away since childhood), and for a way to express that faith in a meaningful, adult way—hence a need to create symbolic, meaningful new rituals.

Symbols play a very important part in the way we experience rituals and they can have both positive and negative effects. The "Ghost of Christmas Past" is a negative symbol of unpleasant, painful memories. It lurks in the shadows like an old "bogey man" intent on spoiling things in the present. It can and it will ruin it for you unless you erase the old images.

How? Whatever the "ghosts" still lurking from the past, bring them into the light of today. Say to them, "That's how it used to be, but that's not how it's going to be!" Plan on small changes at first. Decide to do some things differently. Talk it over with your family. It could be something as simple as putting your Christmas tree in a different corner. It could be as simple as releasing a balloon, watching it float up and away carrying the past with it. It could be as simple as helping the local food bank distribute Christmas baskets, or taking blankets and sleeping bags to homeless shelters.

Perhaps it could be as simple as going to church this Christmas.

# 51

# It's the Thought that Counts!

As we go about the shopping malls, hearing Christmas Carols, looking at the holiday displays, checking our shopping list, what thoughts are roaming around in our heads? Are we too busy about too many "things?" Are we allowing the hustle and bustle of Holiday preparations crowd out the "real thing"—that is, the real message, meaning and gift of Christmas?

Christmas itself is a gift. It is a special gift of time—time set apart from the rest of the year. A time to reflect on the meaning of love, of family, of community, of God and how all this manifests in our lives.

Sometimes we hear people talking about the "commercializing" of Christmas, that the merchants are thinking only of the money they can make during this season, or that people are grasping and greedy and that the "real" message of Christmas is lost in all this material "stuff."

Is that really true? Maybe I'm a hopeless Pollyanna, but I don't think so. The real message of Christmas is Love and one of the many ways we can express love is by giving. Look again at the Christmas displays. Whether they portray a nativity scene, a Santa scene, or a cozy family scene aren't they all sending out messages of love, of caring and sharing? Idealistic perhaps, but we can hardly miss the message if we have eyes to see it. Sure, the display scenes are meant to sell merchandise, but they are also there to assist us in our own "thoughtful" giving.

I'm not proposing that it is wise or prudent to spend beyond one's means and go into debt for months because of Christmas giving. I'm talking about the thought behind the giving.

One of my most precious gifts was a little refrigerator magnet from a granddaughter which says "Happiness is having a grandma like you." One I especially enjoyed giving was a little Hummel figurine to a son. The gift had a special message only he and I understood, one which brought us both to tears.

These two gifts are at the opposite ends of the cost spectrum, yet I couldn't tell you which meant more. "It's the thought that counts!"

Without the magic of giving each year—the act of giving to those we love—the act of contributing to those less fortunate—the magic moment as we open a Christmas card from someone we haven't heard from in a while—we might lose forever the messages of love, hope, peace, joy and connectedness which are such an important part of the celebration of Christmas.

We are physical beings living in a physical world and Christmas can teach us, and perhaps remind us, that we are also spiritual beings and a part of a spiritual world. Our loving acts of giving—whether a material gift or a gift of our time, thought, kindness, prayer and consideration—can help bridge the gap between those two worlds.

There's a feeling of "oneness" at such special times that transcends all understanding. We can't explain it—it just IS.

The feelings of love and connectedness between each other and with God are the essence of the Christmas Spirit. As we busily go about planning and preparing for Christmas for ourselves and our loved ones, be they near or far, let us always keep in mind, "It's the thought that counts." For we really are "our brother's keeper." That little plate of cookies baked for a shut-in, may be the most meaningful gift of that person's Christmas, with an impact we may never know or even suspect.

May we always remember "the Reason for the Season." May we also borrow and adopt a line from Charles Dickens' *A Christmas Carol*—

**I will honor Christmas in my heart and try to keep it all the year.**

# 52

# The Wonderful, Meaningful Symbols of Christmas

There are so many things we take for granted without ever looking into their deeper meaning. How much richer life could be if we understood the origin or history behind some of our most cherished customs and traditions.

As we "deck the halls with boughs of holly" do we understand the symbolism behind what we are doing and what meanings lie hidden beneath these symbols? A definition of a symbol includes an image, a sign, an art object, a decoration, that represents an idea or abstract concept calling forth a response from us on a deep emotional level—evoking feelings not easily or adequately expressed in words. They have an aura of mystery and awe about them. The American flag is not just a red, white and blue cloth blowing in the wind. It is a patriotic symbol representing our country.

So what do the many symbols of Christmas represent? Consider the Christmas tree, the pine, or cedar wreaths. Why were these evergreen boughs chosen to decorate our homes? Because they are "ever green"—remain green all year—and thus became symbols to represent eternal life. The Christmas trees of old had real candles on them. Candles give off light in the darkness—symbols of eternal light. The bulbs on our electric Christmas light strings are shaped like candle flames and have become substitutes for candles because of fire hazard. The symbolism, however, remains the same.

Bells symbolize the "ringing out" of news and were the original "media announcers." They were rung to announce births, weddings, funerals, church services, emergencies, important meetings—all the important events in the life of a community. The town crier rang a bell as he rode about on horseback shouting out the latest news. The Christmas bell announces the "good news" of the birth of Christ.

The nativity scenes retell the story of that first Christmas two thousand years ago. They illustrate for us again the New Testament story as described in the Gospel of Saint Luke—the manger scene with Mary, Joseph and the infant Jesus surrounded by the animals, the shepherds and the angels praising God.

Even that beloved roly-poly figure of Santa Claus has its origin as a religious symbol. He represents St. Nicholas, a Bishop who went about the countryside of Europe a few hundred years ago at Christmas time delivering gifts to needy children.

Let us not get lost in the tinsel and outer trappings of Christmas. Let us allow these symbols of Christmas to reach out and grab our minds and hearts. Let us remember how it felt when we were children—the mystery—the awe—the wonder. Let each of us become that child again and allow these symbols to tell their wonderful stories. Let us share them with our families, especially the little ones. May we all ponder them in our minds and hearts, internalize their meanings and keep the awe, mystery and wonder alive for future generations.